The **Official DVSA Guide** to
Better Driving

Dr Lisa Dorn

Dr Lisa Dorn is an Associate Professor of Driver Behaviour at Cranfield University and past president of the Transportation and Traffic Psychology Division of the International Association of Applied Psychology. Lisa is a Fellow and Chartered member of the Chartered Institute of Ergonomics and Human Factors and a Chartered member of the British Psychological Society.

She has published extensively on the topic of driver behaviour and received the Prince Michael International Award for Road Safety for her work with Arriva and Thames Valley Police and, more recently, for the development of a global fleet safety management programme.

She founded PsyDrive in 2022 as a specialist provider of training for road safety professionals and research, assessment and interventions for improved road safety.

Better Driving is also available as an e-learning course

London: TSO

Published with the permission of the Driver and Vehicle Standards Agency on behalf of the Controller of His Majesty's Stationery Office.

© Crown copyright 2024. All rights reserved. No part of this publication may be reproduced in any material form without the written permission of the copyright owner except in accordance with the provisions of the Copyright, Designs and Patents Act 1988 or under the terms of a licence issued by the Copyright Licensing Agency Ltd. Crown Copyright material is reproduced with permission of the Keeper of the Public Record.

First published 2015
Third edition 2024
Second impression 2025

ISBN 978 0 11554126 1

A CIP catalogue record for this book is available from the British Library

Other titles in the Driving Skills series

The Official DVSA Guide to Driving – the essential skills
The Official DVSA Theory Test for Car Drivers
The Official DVSA Guide to Learning to Drive
The Official DVSA Guide to Better Driving

The Official DVSA Theory Test Kit iPhone/Android app
The Official DVSA Highway Code iPhone/Android app
The Official DVSA Hazard Perception Practice iPhone/Android app

The Official DVSA Guide to Riding – the essential skills
The Official DVSA Theory Test for Motorcyclists
The Official DVSA Guide to Learning to Ride

The Official DVSA Guide to Driving Buses and Coaches
The Official DVSA Guide to Driving Goods Vehicles
The Official DVSA Theory Test for Drivers of Large Vehicles

The Official DVSA Guide to Tractor and Specialist Vehicle Driving Tests (e-book)

Every effort has been made to ensure that the information contained in this publication is accurate at the time of going to press. The Stationery Office cannot be held responsible for any inaccuracies. Information in this book is for guidance only.

The inclusion of advertisements does not imply endorsement of any featured product or organisation by the Department for Transport, the Driver and Vehicle Standards Agency or The Stationery Office (TSO) Limited.

All metric and imperial conversions in this book are approximate.

Please keep up to date with all the latest transport information (particularly technology-driven change) at GOV.UK

DVSA gratefully acknowledges the input of all reviewers, including Professor Gemma Briggs, Professor of Applied Cognitive Psychology at The Open University and Craig Arnold, UN Technical Lead, TRL.

Cover image credit: Krakenimages.com

SD000245

www.carbonbalancedprint.com
CBP2223

We're turning over a new leaf.

MIX
Paper | Supporting responsible forestry
FSC® C002151

Find us online

GOV.UK

GOV.UK is the best place to find government services and information for

- car drivers
- motorcyclists
- driving licences
- driving and riding tests
- towing a caravan or trailer
- medical rules
- driving and riding for a living
- online services.

Visit **www.gov.uk** and try it out.

You can also find contact details for DVSA and other motoring agencies like DVLA at **www.gov.uk**

You'll notice that links to **GOV.UK**, the UK's central government site, do not always take you to a specific page. This is because this kind of site constantly adapts to what people really search for and static links would quickly go out of date. Try it out. Simply search what you need from your preferred search site or from **www.gov.uk** and you should find what you're looking for. You can give feedback to the Government Digital Service from the website.

For readers in Northern Ireland, you can find government services and information online at **nidirect.gov.uk/motoring**

Message from Mark Winn, the Chief Driving Examiner

Good driving is not just about control of the car and knowing the rules of the road – it's also about being a responsible driver and coping with the traffic situations you'll meet. Developing that responsibility comes, in part, with experience. But it's also about your personal approach. For example, do you think you set a good example while you're driving – to your passengers (particularly children), and other road users?

We all start out knowing how to drive well – otherwise how would we have passed the test? We know that things like using a mobile phone while driving and speeding are not good. But bad habits can creep in. We may become over-confident – or lose confidence; for example, after a near-miss or when in-car technology and The Highway Code change.

A good driver is just as aware of their faults as they are of their abilities, so you've scored on that measure by picking up this book. 'Better Driving' explains how your attitude, mood, health and other factors can affect the way you behave at the wheel. We invite you to reflect on your style of driving and to consider how you can improve on that style.

We hope this book helps you to find your own unique way to become a better driver. You could be rewarded with lower costs, more confidence and enjoyment, and less stress. You'll also set a great example to your passengers and other road users. Most importantly, we hope it will help you towards a lifetime of safe driving.

Mark Winn

Mark Winn
Chief Driving Examiner

The Driver and Vehicle Standards Agency (DVSA) is an executive agency of the Department for Transport.

We improve road safety in Great Britain by setting standards for driving and motorcycling, and making sure drivers, vehicle operators and MOT garages understand and follow roadworthiness standards. We also provide a range of licensing, testing, education and enforcement services.

www.gov.uk/dvsa

The Driver and Vehicle Agency (DVA) is an executive agency within the Department for Infrastructure for Northern Ireland.

Its primary aim is to promote and improve road safety through the advancement of driving standards and implementation of the government's policies for improving the mechanical standards of vehicles.

nidirect.gov.uk/motoring

Contents

Message from Mark Winn, the Chief Driving Examiner — 5

Introduction — 9

Section one – The human factors in driving — 12

You, the driver — 13
How you process information — 15
Your mental landscape — 23
Risk perception — 28
Confidence — 33
Your personality — 40
Stress, mood and emotions — 45
Summary — 56

Section two – Other influences on your driving — 58

Distractions — 59
Fatigue — 66
Alcohol and drugs — 69
New technologies — 76
The road environment — 87
Summary — 88

Section three – Developing better strategies — 90

Feeling nervous about driving — 91
Coping with challenging scenarios — 95
Learner drivers and managing anxiety — 108
Driving offences — 111
Driving as you get older — 113
Improving your reaction to stress — 116
Summary — 118

Section four – Refresh your knowledge   **120**

The changing road environment	121
The hierarchy of road users	127
Speed limits	130
Motorway driving	135
Vehicle maintenance and breakdowns	140
Summary	144

Section five – The way forward   **146**

What's next for UK roads?	147
What's next for UK drivers?	148
Automated technology and your driving skills	153
An ongoing process	155

Photographic credits   162

Appendix: The national standard for driving   163

Selected bibliography   166

Index   172

Introduction

You can improve your driving skills and hazard perception through practice under the guidance of an approved driving instructor (ADI). However, responsibility for improving your **behavioural skills** lies with you. This is because driving **skill** relates to your ability to manoeuvre your car safely in traffic, whereas your **behaviour** depends on psychological factors: it's an outcome of your lifestyle, personality, motivations and temperament.

This book will help you to understand yourself as a driver and give you the techniques you need to address your personal risk from a behavioural perspective. You'll not only become a better driver but also boost your confidence levels and increase your enjoyment of driving.

Driving skills vs driver behaviour – what's the difference?

It's important to understand the difference between 'driver behaviour' and 'driving skills'. Driver behaviour does not refer to the manual skills you need to drive your vehicle safely. Rather, it means the way you choose to use those driving skills in the traffic environment and your personality and emotional state when you come to drive.

Most incidents are the result of poor driver behaviour. Typical behaviours that increase risk include

- a bad decision by the driver – for example, going through traffic lights as they turn red
- not paying enough attention to what's going on around you
- unsafe speed choices
- not leaving enough space between your vehicle and other road users
- using a mobile phone while driving.

> **!** **Remember**
> The way you behave as a driver is influenced by your thoughts and feelings.

Who is this book for?

This book will benefit all drivers, but it's especially relevant to

- those who are returning to driving after a break, to update you on the knowledge and skills you need to drive safely
- anyone looking to drive for their job, or increasing their mileage for work
- drivers who've recently been convicted of a traffic offence, to help you reflect on the reasons you committed the offence and work out how to improve your driving in the future
- nervous drivers looking to develop strategies to improve their confidence levels
- older drivers, to help you evaluate your driving and reduce your risk
- driving instructors, as supporting material in your understanding of the human aspects of driving
- anyone interested in the psychological aspects of driving.

How is the book structured?

To help you get the most from the book, you'll find

Self-reflection
These boxes get you thinking about your driving.

Tip
Tips and strategies for safer driving.

Science boxes to help you understand how you process information when you drive.

Key information about driving and the law.

There are also

Facts
These boxes have important information to help you learn.

Remember
These boxes help you keep essential tips and techniques in mind.

Links to other resources.

Definitions boxes to help explain important terms.

In addition, you'll find
- evidence-based assessments to help you discover how your mind works and how this might affect your driving
- scenario-based learning, to help you understand how you typically respond in certain situations, and reflect on how you could improve
- diagrams and images.

Life-long learning

Many drivers assume that passing their driving test means they have the necessary knowledge and skills to drive through to old age, but there can be many challenges to overcome along the way. You may be reading this book because you're having some difficulties with your driving for one reason or another. You may not have driven for a while and need to get up to date with how to drive on today's roads. You may have particular concerns or simply want to learn something new to be a better driver.

Most people never receive any additional driver training after passing their driving test and may feel ill-equipped for today's roads. The good news is that this is nothing unusual – from time to time everyone feels the same. Safe driving is a life-long process of discovery and there's always something new to learn. Nobody can ever know everything, but the tools and techniques you'll find in this book will help you become a better and safer driver.

Section one

The human factors in driving

In this section, you'll learn about

- driving and your mental workload
- how thoughts, feelings and beliefs affect your behaviour at the wheel
- how to reflect on the way you drive
- thrill-seeking tendencies and their effects on your driving
- how angry and stressed driving affects your safety
- how to deal with driving under pressure.

You, the driver

If you were to write down the most important factors in driver safety, what would be on your list? It's likely that you'd mention your skill as a driver, the rules of the road and the actions of other road users. You'd be right, too – all of these have a major influence on your driving. What you might not mention is the single most important factor of all: you, the driver.

The way you think about driving and the way you feel when you come to drive can be described as the 'human factors' in driver safety. Six of the main human factors that can affect your driving performance are

1. How you process information – how do your brain and eyes work while you're driving?
2. Your 'mental landscape' – how do your thoughts and feelings affect your driving decisions?
3. Risk perception – how do you assess road risk and how is this affected by your beliefs about what might happen?
4. Confidence – how does your belief in your ability and skills influence your driving decisions and risk taking?
5. Your personality – how do your thrill-seeking tendencies influence the way you drive?
6. Stress, mood and emotions – how do your feelings, including anger and nervousness, affect your ability to drive safely?

Self-reflection
Think about the questions in the list above. How would you answer them?

Defensive driving

Before we take a closer look at how human factors affect the way we drive, it's important to mention that becoming a better driver requires a defensive approach to driving. Defensive driving goes beyond the mechanics of handling a vehicle and understanding the rules of the road. Its aim is to reduce your risk of collision by anticipating potentially dangerous situations.

In particular, defensive driving involves
- awareness
- anticipation
- planning
- staying in control.

It also means driving with
- responsibility
- care
- consideration and courtesy.

This can be achieved by practising specific driving techniques that are covered in this book and in 'The Official DVSA Guide to Driving – the essential skills'.

Defensive driving means reducing the dangers associated with driving, by heightening your awareness of everything that's happening around you. It means controlling the way you think and feel and not being negatively affected by the behaviour of other road users. As a defensive driver, you quickly identify potential problems on the road and immediately decide on the best course of action.

Take this approach to driving and you'll be a better and safer driver – particularly if you acknowledge that an element of risk is involved every time you get in a car.

How you process information

Most of the information that your brain processes while you're driving is visual. This includes
- information from the road environment
- other vehicles
- pedestrians
- road signs
- the scenery you're passing.

You may be processing information from other sources at the same time – for example, listening to music or talking with a passenger. You may also be thinking about where you're going or planning what you'll do once you arrive.

External and internal inputs like these bombard your brain with information. When you're driving, you must select the most important information to avoid making mistakes. There are simply not enough mental resources available to carry out all the tasks at the same time.

Driving is particularly difficult when
- the information flow becomes a torrent (for example, you're driving fast)
- the information is of low quality (for example, visibility is poor because you're driving at night or in bad weather)
- resources must be focused on a particular piece of information (for example, a hazard captures your attention)
- your mental capacity is reduced (for example, due to drugs, alcohol, stress or fatigue).

Most road traffic collisions happen when critical information was available but went unnoticed. For example, you may have failed to notice and act upon this information because your mental resources were focused elsewhere. In other words, you were distracted.

An imperfect system

The brain is a complex organ and can make mistakes when interpreting the world around us. Our eyes are able to capture only a small fraction of the visual information that's available, so the brain fills in the gaps and makes assumptions.

The way we process information is also extremely limited. We can only attend to a small amount of the information we receive, from which we make our decisions and respond. All the other information that's available either goes unnoticed or slips from memory.

We can only attend to small amounts of the visual information we receive

There's always the possibility that we'll miss a hazard unless we look directly at it. Even then, there's no guarantee that we'll respond to it, as we often look but fail to see a hazard because the brain has not processed the potential for the hazard to unfold.

 Self-reflection
Have you ever been at a junction, looked and not seen a cyclist or motorcyclist?

 For an example of how the brain selectively processes information, have a look at this video.

youtube.com/watch?v=vJG698U2Mvo

Once your brain has decided to take action – for example, to brake – it takes about three-quarters of a second for your body to react and move your foot from the accelerator to the brake pedal. You may travel up to 31 metres (100 feet) during that time, depending on your speed – and this assumes that your reaction times are not impaired by other human factors, such as fatigue or the effects of alcohol.

Remember
Do not forget the rule that thinking distance + braking distance = stopping distance. At 70 mph, you travel 31 metres (about 3 coach lengths) every second.

Thinking distance (distance travelled in the time it takes to react to a situation) **+** **Braking distance** (distance travelled from when you start to use the brakes to when your car completely stops) **=** **Stopping distance**

The science of hazard perception

The way the brain functions when anticipating the threat from developing hazards may be responsible for the difference in risk between an experienced driver and a novice driver.

Imagine you're driving and you suddenly notice a pedestrian stepping out in front of you. Even with just a hint of movement in your peripheral vision, your full attention is guided towards the hazard. Your brain does not waste time telling its 'thinking part' that the pedestrian is about to step into the path of your car and that you should brake.

Your visual cortex (the part of your brain that receives and processes what your eyes take in) feeds the information to the brainstem (the part of the brain that's attached to the spinal cord). This information is then sent on to the area of the brain that controls movement. At this point, your foot moves to touch the brake. This is an automatic response based on past experience. It's thought that our brain leaves a 'marker' whenever it encounters a threat, allowing it to respond more quickly when the same kind of scenario occurs again.

Why is this important? Well, there's evidence to suggest that this 'automated response' allows experienced drivers to react earlier to hazards. The process only seems to develop with repeated exposure to different hazards and road situations. This could explain why experienced drivers are better able to avoid risky situations than inexperienced drivers.

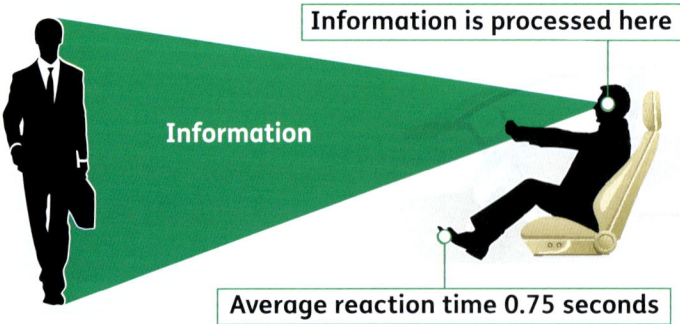

Self-reflection

How good are your hazard perception skills?

How good do you think your hazard perception skills are? Studies have found that drivers have virtually no insight into how good they are at recognising and responding to hazards. In fact, these studies tell us that drivers often judge their hazard perception skills to be far better than they actually are. This may be due to the traffic environment being quite forgiving of the errors we make. In other words, when we fail to see a hazard, other road users can take avoiding action and compensate for our mistake.

Hazard perception is a core driving skill. How many of these hazards would you have recognised if they were not circled?

To learn more about practising your hazard perception skills, visit the Safe Driving for Life website and take a look at 'The Official DVSA Guide to Hazard Perception Online'.

safedrivingforlife.info/shop/official-dvsa-guide-hazard-perception-elearning/

Distractions

With so many in-car gadgets, distraction is now even more of a problem for drivers. Most of us will have changed the radio station while driving and come through unscathed, so we may wonder whether the presence of these technologies really compromises our safety. Well, the **extent** to which a driver is distracted depends on the type of task, **when** it's performed and **how long** it takes to complete. Short tasks that require an easy response (such as pressing a button) do not demand much of the brain, but longer tasks that require a response to a menu (programming a sat nav or using a mobile phone, for example) are **very** demanding and should not be attempted on the move.

THINK! road safety campaign poster showing the effects of distracted driving.

 Remember
Do not allow any distraction, large or small, to compromise safety.

Who gets distracted?

Younger, inexperienced drivers and older drivers are more vulnerable than others to the distracting effects of technology – but for different reasons.

- For young drivers, distraction is due to a greater inclination to engage in risk-taking behaviour, such as using a mobile phone while driving. This is because the risk of doing so is not considered or recognised.
- For older drivers, distraction is more likely to be due to a decline in their visual and/or cognitive faculties (meaning anything that relates to mental processes, such as thinking, learning and remembering).

Strategies for dealing with distraction

Ask yourself
- Is there a safe place where you can stop and take stock?
- Do you really need to take that phone call?

Think about
- whether you can use alternative transport to go out with friends
- the type of music you're playing (see section 2 for more information) and how loud it is. If the volume is too high, it might start to affect your driving.

Self-reflection scenario
You're on a night out with your friends and are now driving them home after midnight. They've been drinking and are arguing loudly.

Ask yourself
- How can you make sure that you get everyone home safely?
- What could you do to make sure your passengers do not distract you?

Strategies for safer driving
- Focus on the road, not on what's happening in the car.
- Ask your passengers to quieten down so you do not make any mistakes.
- Be confident enough to say you need to make sure everyone gets home safely.
- Talk to your passengers in a friendly way so you do not upset anyone.
- Tell them you need to concentrate – especially when driving in the dark.

Mental workload

Some driving tasks create a greater mental workload than others. Junctions can be particularly challenging in terms of the amount of information you have to process. At a junction you need to make a solid assessment of the speed and distance of oncoming vehicles, sometimes in both directions. You also need to look out for pedestrians and cyclists. Other vehicles may be queuing behind you and this may make you feel anxious, as you want to avoid keeping other road users waiting too long.

Ask yourself

- How long do you spend looking at junctions?
- Are you always sure that you've judged the speed and distance of oncoming traffic correctly?
- Have you checked for cyclists and motorcyclists?

You should make sure that you check the blind spots. Smaller vehicles take up less space in your visual field and might be overlooked.

Many collisions are caused by a failure to correctly judge the speed of oncoming vehicles or work out whether there's a sufficient gap to join the traffic on a main road. On average, drivers spend just 0.5 seconds visually searching at junctions.

Remember
Keeping on top of your ability to anticipate, detect and respond to hazards is a core skill for drivers.

Your mental landscape

As we saw in the introduction, there's a difference between 'driver behaviour' and 'driver skill'. Driver behaviour is influenced by motives, attitudes, emotional responses to traffic, personality traits, lifestyle, etc, whereas driver skill is related to your ability behind the wheel. This includes your knowledge of The Highway Code and your technical skills in manoeuvring the vehicle. It's possible to have excellent driving skills but very poor driving behaviour.

Driving is an activity that gives you a large element of control over how you interact with your vehicle and other road users. The main goal in driving is to reach a destination, but this ultimate goal comprises many other associated goals, such as reaching the destination quickly, comfortably, enjoyably and safely. In order to fulfil these goals, a wide range of tasks must be performed by you, the driver. You need to have the right mental skills to perform these tasks well.

Driving, thinking and feeling

The way you **think** and **feel** affects how well you drive. Your thoughts and feelings have an impact on how vulnerable you are to internal and external sources of distraction while driving. For example, feeling stressed about being late might make you more prone to mental distraction. Your thoughts and feelings also affect your hazard perception skills. For example, driving too fast because you think you're not at risk will mean that you're less able to perceive hazards, given the increased information flow.

Remember
Your thoughts and feelings are reflected in your behaviour when you drive. Negative emotions, anger, anxiety and frustration can all compromise your safety and must be addressed if you're to become a better driver.

What are you thinking?

Your beliefs or ways of thinking are fairly consistent patterns of thoughts or 'attitudes' that determine the way you interpret or make sense of what's going on around you and the behaviour of other road users. To become a safer and more confident driver, you need to understand the beliefs and thought patterns that underpin the way you drive.

Remember
It's not the traffic events themselves that determine how you feel and act – it's the way you interpret and evaluate those events.

You may not be aware of the perceptions and expectations you hold. You may not have even questioned whether the way you think about other road users is valid. These 'hazards in the mind' can lead to intentional or unintentional risk taking. For example, you may believe that drivers who 'cut you up' are doing so deliberately. This way of thinking might lead you to drive faster or react angrily to a driver who does this, to teach them a lesson. Some road users may end up feeling intimidated to the point where they no longer wish to drive.

How are you feeling?

While you may not be consciously aware of the way you think and how this influences your driving behaviour, you can be consciously aware of how you feel when driving. You may find yourself acting on your feelings and expressing them behind the wheel without linking these feelings with your thought processes. Your feelings are an essential part of your decision making as a driver.

Consider the example of the driver cutting you up. Your way of thinking meant that you interpreted this as a hostile act, which then led to feelings of annoyance. If you think that other drivers should never cut you up (belief), you're likely to feel angry if they do (feelings). Feeling angry can affect your decision making by directing your attention exclusively towards the driver who broke your rule. Instantly, your brain tells you to retaliate. This can swamp your ability to process other critical information and, as a result, it increases your risk.

Assess your way of thinking and feeling

There's a clear link between your thought processes, your feelings and your behaviour. In order to discover this link, you need to reflect and gain insight into the way your mind works when you're driving.

Driver beliefs and feelings can take many forms. It's impossible to list them all, but you can ask yourself what some of your beliefs might be and how they affect the way you feel.

Sometimes the way you feel as a driver can affect your thought processes. At the same time, the way you feel in response to driving-related events helps to develop your beliefs.

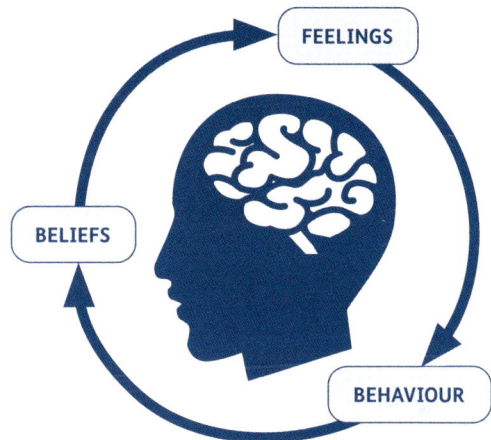

Our beliefs, feelings and driving behaviours are all connected.

As an example of how this works in practice, think about a situation in your driving life that has made you feel very anxious. Can you identify what thought processes are underpinning your nervousness? What's at the root of your worries? Perhaps you **believe** you're not skilled enough to deal with, say, bad weather on a motorway? Perhaps you worry about large vehicles driving too close?

Once you've identified the way that your thought processes are affecting the way you feel, you can take action to change the way you look at different road and traffic situations. This will help to reduce your anxiety. More practical guidance on this can be found in section 3.

You can also try to separate your thoughts and feelings from your driving skills. Ask yourself: if you were not so nervous, would you be able to drive better? This will help you to identify whether you need to address your beliefs about your driving and increase your confidence or whether you genuinely need to improve your driving skills. In both circumstances, an approved driving instructor (ADI) can help you.

Self-reflection and driving ability

Feedback is critical to developing your driving. Imagine if your driving instructor did not give you any feedback when you made mistakes during your driving lesson. Without your driving instructor correcting faulty decisions, you could easily develop bad habits and drive in a way that puts you and other road users at risk.

You need to develop your self-awareness and provide feedback to yourself throughout your driving life. Being able to reflect on your thought processes and your emotional reactions to driving will provide that feedback and help you to improve.

Self-reflection scenario

The last time you took your car out, someone drove too close behind you and sounded their horn to get you to move out of the way. They overtook you and you could see they were shouting at you as they passed by at speed. You felt very annoyed at the time and you were distracted from driving for a few minutes afterwards as you thought about what happened.

To self-reflect, start by replaying this scenario in your head, but this time really focus on your thoughts and feelings while you were driving.

- What was it about this situation that made you feel annoyed? Was it because of the increased risk in the situation? Was it because you felt the other driver was out of order? There might be a number of other reasons but only you can answer this question.
- Once you know what was at the root of your anger, you'll understand yourself better.
- By understanding what makes you angry, you have more control over how you choose to respond.
- You can choose to make sure the behaviour of other road users does not distract you from driving safely.

Triggers for self-reflection

To become better drivers, we have to recognise the triggers that tell us it's time for self-reflection. Broadly, triggers for self-reflection occur when you're surprised by another driver's actions or find yourself getting angry or nervous.

Think about the last time you got annoyed with another driver, then consider the following questions.
- What was the point of your journey?
- Were you in a hurry?
- What was going on in your mind before you got annoyed?
- Were you already in a bad mood?
- Did you think that this particular road user was not following the rules of the road?
- Is it realistic to expect all road users to follow the traffic rules all the time?
- How did it make you feel when the other driver failed to do things properly?
- Was it useful to get annoyed because of the other driver's actions?
- Were you already feeling under pressure before the event took place?
- Did you drive close to the other driver to teach them a lesson or make aggressive gestures? If so, how did your response increase the risk of an incident taking place?
- Looking back, what could you have done differently to reduce any risk in that situation?
- How can you make more of an allowance for other road users' mistakes next time?

If your thoughts, feelings and beliefs have such an effect on the way you drive, is there any way you can deal with negative responses to certain situations? The answer is yes, because driver behaviour is primarily learned. This means that faulty beliefs can be challenged through self-reflection.

Next steps
- Through self-reflection, develop a strategy for how to reduce your risk in the future.
- Think about how you could make safer decisions next time.

Risk perception

One of the human factors that can have a strong impact on the way you choose to drive is how you perceive risk.

There are surprisingly few collisions on the road, considering how much traffic there is. In fact, your chances of being involved in an incident on any one trip are close to zero. Unfortunately, if you rarely see a collision, this can lead you to believe that it's not always necessary to follow the rules of the road.

If you believe there's little chance that you'll have a crash, then you're more likely to take risks and increase your statistical risk by the way you choose to drive. Driving too quickly will increase your risk relative to other road users.

On the other hand, if you believe you're highly likely to be involved in an incident, then your perception of risk is much greater. You'd be more likely to drive with extreme caution to avoid what you judge to be the inevitable crash.

It's clear that there are strong individual differences in our perception of risk, with some people underestimating and others overestimating the risk. This belief in your chances of being involved in an incident has an important effect on your behaviour, so it's worth considering in more detail.

Your driving safety bubble

Some researchers believe that, on a day-to-day basis, drivers rarely think about risk at all. Instead, they maintain space around their car at a level they're comfortable with. (This is often referred to as the personal safety margin.) Driving soon becomes an unconscious habitual activity based on maintaining this safety bubble.

Some drivers' safety bubbles are too small. These drivers tend to enter other people's safety bubbles – for example, by travelling too close to the vehicle in front. This makes other drivers feel uncomfortable and, worse still, increases the risk of incidents.

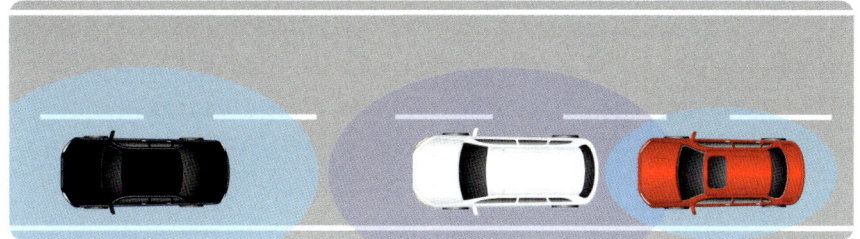

In this diagram, the red car has entered the white car's safety bubble. This is because the driver of the red car has an incorrect perception of the 'safe distance' from the car in front.

Optimism bias

Optimism bias is a kind of distortion in the way you perceive risk. It causes you to believe that you're less at risk of being involved in an incident than other drivers. It's a general belief that leads you into thinking that you can expect to have a more positive experience of driving than others. The danger with this way of thinking is that you may not follow the rules of the road if you think you're not going to be involved in an incident in the first place.

While young drivers as a group are more likely to drive dangerously and be involved in road traffic collisions, not all young drivers have an optimistic bias and high-risk tendencies. Some young drivers have a strong aversion to risk and consider that their risk of being involved in a crash is high. You may hold a pessimistic bias that a negative event is highly likely to happen to you. This way of thinking can lead to anxiety, which can affect your driving performance in different ways.

Self-reflection

Think about it. How big is your safety bubble?

How close do you drive to vehicles in front of you? How close are you prepared to drive to vehicles alongside you? What if you needed to brake sharply? Could you stop in time?

How optimistic are you about your driving experiences?

Self-reflection scenario

You're driving on a dual carriageway in heavy traffic. The traffic is preventing you from driving as fast as you'd like to drive. Generally, you like to be driving at around the speed limit of the road you're on. You're just a couple of metres from the car in front and staring blankly ahead. Suddenly, the line of traffic comes to a complete standstill and you narrowly avoid going into the back of the car in front.

Ask yourself

- How could you avoid this scenario in the future?
- Think about your habit of driving at the speed limit of the road you're on. How could you prepare better for unexpected events?
- In which situations are you most likely to drive without being properly aware of what's going on?

Strategies for safer driving

- Review your perception of risk in this situation – was it over-optimistic for the circumstances?
- Stay aware of the dangers of driving 'on automatic pilot'.
- Be aware of the brake lights on vehicles ahead of you to allow for a smooth reaction. Braking should be progressive – in other words, steadily increased, not sudden.
- Follow the 'two-second rule' and leave a safe gap.
- Make sure you allow larger gaps in bad weather and when driving at night to allow for longer braking times and poorer visibility.
- Look around and through the windows of the vehicles ahead of you, as far as the road horizon, to check for brake lights coming on further up the line of traffic. This will help you to anticipate what action might be required in good time.
- Look in your mirrors and scan to the sides frequently.
- You may need to move your head and body or slightly alter your car's position to get a better look.
- Check your speed regularly – it's very easy to increase your speed without realising it, and this will close the gap between you and the vehicle ahead.

As drivers we are relatively poor at estimating risk, for a number of reasons

1. You get little feedback on your risk taking because risky behaviours can be performed regularly with no consequences. This is because forgiveness for errors and violations is built into the traffic system. (See section 4 for more about how vehicle and road engineering has helped to improve road safety.) Other road users can often take avoiding action when you do something wrong. It's only when a certain combination of factors occurs that an incident takes place. A collision is often the result of the actions of more than one party and you may not be prepared to accept blame for your own actions. We have a strong human tendency to blame other road users and fail to acknowledge the role we played in an incident.
2. Also, our capacity to recall risky experiences, such as near misses is poor. As a result, you're unlikely to learn from your mistakes and will have a tendency to repeat them.
3. You tend to believe you're more likely to experience a positive event than a negative one (optimism bias).

You can use this understanding of the way we all perceive risk to be a better driver.

Self-reflection

What do you think are your chances of being involved in a collision in the next 12 months?

Compared with other drivers, how likely do you think it is that you'll be involved in a collision in the next 12 months?

Now, let's reflect on those 2 points further.

If you think there's little chance of being involved in a collision in the next 12 months, ask yourself whether this is a realistic assessment. 'It won't happen to me' is an example of optimism bias that may hinder your ability to estimate risk and compromise your safety and the safety of other road users.

If there's a big difference between your rating of your own risk and your rating of the risk for other drivers, ask yourself whether this difference is realistic. Is your driving really that much better than other people's?

Whether your self-rating is realistic or unrealistic is difficult to determine. Most drivers judge themselves to have less than a 10% probability of being involved in a crash. If you're a new driver, your actual risk is around 20% in the first year of driving.

If you think you're very likely to be involved in a crash then perhaps you need to question whether your confidence levels are too low or whether you need to develop your driving skills, or both.

Confidence

Newly licensed drivers often become overconfident in their abilities soon after passing their driving test, despite their lack of experience. For example, studies of novice drivers have shown that they're inclined to be excessively confident in their ability to predict the behaviour of other road users. This makes them feel justified in taking risks such as speeding or tailgating. Novice drivers also tend to believe they can control the traffic situation to a greater extent than is realistic given the amount of driving experience they have.

How skilful a driver are you?

Have a look at the following table and estimate how much skill you have in each of the following aspects of driving. Use this scale:

0 – **Well below average**
1 – **Below average**
2 – **About average**
3 – **Above average**
4 – **Well above average**

	Below average		Average	Above average	
	0	1	2	3	4
Management of your car in heavy traffic					
Performance in a critical situation					
Hazard perception in traffic					
Driving in a strange city					
Keeping to the traffic rules					

	Below average		Aver- age	Above average	
	0	1	2	3	4
Managing the car through a skid					
Predicting traffic situations ahead					
Driving carefully					
Knowing how to act in particular traffic situations					
Fluent lane-changing in heavy traffic					
Fast reactions					
Making firm decisions					
Paying attention to other road users					
Driving fast if necessary					
Driving in the dark					
Controlling the vehicle					
Avoiding competition in traffic					
Keeping sufficient following distance					
Adjusting your speed to the conditions					
Overtaking					

	Below average		Average	Above average	
	0	1	2	3	4
Keeping to the speed limits					
Avoiding unnecessary risks					
Tolerating other drivers' mistakes calmly					
Obeying the traffic lights					

How did you score?

You may have scored yourself highly in some of these areas and perhaps not so highly in others. Look carefully at those areas where you've scored yourself as above average. Are you sure your skills are above average all the time? Are there circumstances under which you're less likely to perform these driving tasks competently? Perhaps you might rate yourself differently when you're in a hurry or in a bad mood?

Whatever your perception of your driving skills, there's often a difference between what you think about your driving and your actual skills. Do not worry, it's not specific to individuals – this disconnect is due to a number of human biases in the way we think. In particular, we have a tendency to misperceive the way traffic events unfold and process information in our favour. These biases might be due to a number of different human factors

1. the tendency to ignore times when you were not driving well
2. a self-serving selection of examples when your driving was skilful
3. the tendency to see what you expect to see
4. the way you were feeling at the time
5. your personality
6. your motivations while driving.

If you rated yourself poorly on driving skills, scoring yourself as below average, an ADI could help you improve both your skills and your confidence.

Understand your driving weaknesses

- Biases in your beliefs about your driving skills are a common human tendency we're mostly unaware of. The first step towards better driving is to acknowledge how biased your view of your driving skills might be.

  The next time another driver is aggressive towards you for making a mistake, instead of automatically defending your actions, consider what element of your driving needs to be improved. For example
  - Were you driving too close?
  - Did you force another driver to brake harshly?
  - Were you driving too fast for the conditions?
  - Did you fail to look in your mirrors and see this road user?

- Improve your driving skills by learning from your mistakes. For example, if you have a near miss after emerging from a junction, the next time you're in that situation, spend longer scanning the road for potential hazards before you move out.

Influencing your mental demands

We all make mistakes when driving. No matter how experienced you are or how well you've been trained, you can still get it wrong. Most drivers try to avoid overloading their ability to process information by regulating the way they drive. You can influence the demands on you as a driver by adjusting your actions.

For example, the faster you drive, the less time you have to process information, to make decisions, to take action and to correct errors – all of which makes your drive more difficult. Multitasking and other distractions, such as talking on a mobile phone (even if it's hands-free) or using a music system, make things even harder.

On the other hand, if you drive at an appropriate speed for the road you're on, you have more time to process information and make safe decisions.

Errors, lapses and violations

Even the best drivers make mistakes, do foolish things or bend the rules at one time or another. Some of these behaviours are trivial, but others are potentially dangerous. Look at each of the following items and think about how often you've done these kinds of things over the past year. Make a mental note of how often you commit errors, lapses and violations.

Error – when we have a plan about how we intend to make a manoeuvre but execute it ineffectively

Lapse – usually due to a failure in your concentration

Violation – a deliberate action that breaks the law.

Attempt to overtake someone you had not noticed to be signalling a right turn	**ERROR**
Get into the wrong lane when approaching a roundabout or a junction	**LAPSE**
Miss 'stop' or 'give way' signs and narrowly avoid colliding with traffic having right of way	**ERROR**
Misread the signs and leave a roundabout on the wrong road	**LAPSE**
Fail to notice that pedestrians are crossing when turning into a side street from a main road	**ERROR**
Drive especially close to the car in front as a signal to its driver to go faster or get out of the way	**VIOLATION**
Forget where you left your car in a car park	**LAPSE**
Queuing to turn left onto a main road, you pay such close attention to the main stream of traffic that you nearly hit the car in front	**ERROR**
When reversing, hit something that you had not previously seen	**LAPSE**
Cross a junction knowing that the traffic lights have already turned against you	**VIOLATION**

On turning left, nearly hit a cyclist who has come up on your inside	**ERROR**
Disregard the speed limits late at night or very early in the morning	**VIOLATION**
Attempt to drive away from the traffic lights in third gear	**LAPSE**
Fail to check your rear-view mirror before pulling out, changing lanes, etc	**ERROR**
Have a dislike for a particular class of road user, and show your hostility in any way you can	**VIOLATION**
Become impatient with a slow driver in the outer lane and overtake on the inside	**VIOLATION**
Underestimate the speed of an oncoming vehicle when overtaking	**ERROR**
Switch on one thing, such as the headlights, when you meant to switch on something else, such as the windscreen wipers	**LAPSE**
Brake too quickly on a slippery road, or steer the wrong way in a skid	**ERROR**
Intending to drive to destination A, you 'wake up' to find yourself on the road to destination B, perhaps because B is your more usual destination	**LAPSE**
Drive even though you realise you may be over the legal blood-alcohol limit	**VIOLATION**
Get involved in unofficial 'races' with other drivers	**VIOLATION**
Realise that you have no clear recollection of the road you've just been travelling along	**LAPSE**
Angered by another driver's behaviour, you give chase with the intention of giving him/her a piece of your mind	**VIOLATION**

How did you score?

Look carefully at those areas that apply to you most often.

If you assessed yourself honestly, you'll know that thinking about why you've made a mistake is the first step towards finding out how you can avoid making the same mistake again.

Do not overthink and dwell on your mistakes, though. Learn from them and decide to become a better driver.

Ask yourself: under what circumstances am I more likely to commit errors, lapses and violations? Every time you make a mistake or commit a violation, there's an opportunity to be a better driver by reflecting on the reasons why it happened. These are the triggers for self-reflection discussed earlier in this section.

The ability to self-reflect on personal weaknesses, such as overconfidence in driving skills, is a core skill for all drivers. This is the first step towards acknowledging your weaknesses – which are not necessarily due to poor driving skills, but may instead be due to the belief that your driving skills are above average and that you can therefore afford to take risks. Once you understand how your beliefs about risk and your confidence in your driving skills might influence your driving behaviour, the next step is to recognise this tendency when you're making decisions behind the wheel.

Next steps

- Reflect on the areas where you consider your skills to be above average. Are they realistic?
- Think about the errors, lapses and violations you're likely to commit. For example
    - Perhaps you have a tendency to drive too close to other vehicles in a traffic queue and might go into the back of another car?
    - Perhaps you have a tendency to drive too fast for the circumstances and may lose control of your car?
    - Perhaps you have a tendency to emerge from junctions without looking out for fast-moving vehicles in the far distance?

Once you've thought about these different kinds of scenarios, it's easy to discover how to reduce your risk.

Your personality

Sensation-seeking and thrill-seeking tendencies are personality characteristics with strong links to risk-taking behaviour. That might seem like a difficult thing to get your head around, but it's not quite as complex as it sounds.

'Sensation seeking' is the tendency to look for varied, novel, complex and intense sensations and a willingness to take risks for the sake of experiencing them. For example, that might include playing dangerous sports or using drugs.

'Thrill seeking' is the way in which sensation-seeking tendencies are expressed. On the road, that might mean speeding on unsuitable roads or making risky overtaking manoeuvres.

Thrill-seeking tendencies lead to risk taking, and risk taking increases your chances of being involved in a collision. For example, driving under the influence of alcohol is strongly associated with thrill-seeking tendencies.

Facts
- Drivers in their 20s have the highest rates of drink-driving crashes.
- Young drivers who crash are twice as likely to be impaired by alcohol as older drivers who crash, and this is far more common among young men than among young women.

Test yourself

Are you a thrill-seeking driver? If you are, you can reduce your chances of being involved in a collision. Have a look at the following questionnaire and answer the questions as honestly as you can.

Thrill-seeking questionnaire

Answer the following questions on the basis of your usual or typical feelings about driving.

1. I get a buzz from the whole driving experience

| 0 | 1 | 2 | 3 | 4 | 5 | 6 | 7 | 8 | 9 | 10 |

not at all   very much

2. Safety is less important than the thrill of driving fast

| 0 | 1 | 2 | 3 | 4 | 5 | 6 | 7 | 8 | 9 | 10 |

not at all   very much

3. I get a thrill out of driving fast

| 0 | 1 | 2 | 3 | 4 | 5 | 6 | 7 | 8 | 9 | 10 |

not at all   very much

4. I like to raise my adrenaline levels while driving

| 0 | 1 | 2 | 3 | 4 | 5 | 6 | 7 | 8 | 9 | 10 |

not at all   very much

5. Being a racing driver would be a dream come true

| 0 | 1 | 2 | 3 | 4 | 5 | 6 | 7 | 8 | 9 | 10 |

not at all   very much

6. I sometimes like to frighten myself a little when driving

0	1	2	3	4	5	6	7	8	9	10

not at all   very much

7. I like to drive round corners at speed

0	1	2	3	4	5	6	7	8	9	10

not at all   very much

8. I would love to drive a sports car on a road with no speed limit

0	1	2	3	4	5	6	7	8	9	10

not at all   very much

9. I feel in control when I'm driving fast

0	1	2	3	4	5	6	7	8	9	10

not at all   very much

10. I enjoy the sensation of accelerating rapidly

0	1	2	3	4	5	6	7	8	9	10

not at all   very much

Your results

Add up your score and read the relevant category below to find out more about your thrill-seeking tendencies.

Routine driver (score between 0 and 25)

You prefer a well-ordered and routine style of driving and like to stick to the road rules. You have a traditional view of what driving should be about. For you, driving is not about gaining excitement and enjoying the risks, but taking a steady, calm and structured approach in order to arrive safely.

Low-risk driver (score between 26 and 50)

You tend not to use driving as a source of excitement: you see it more as a way of getting from A to B than as a way to get your adrenaline rush for the day. You usually avoid taking corners at speed or driving fast when there are only a few cars on the road. You generally follow the rules of the road.

Occasional risk taker (score between 51 and 75)

You sometimes enjoy an adrenaline rush when driving fast and taking corners sharply. From time to time you might like to experience a buzz from driving, especially on open country roads with bends and hills. You sometimes like to accelerate rapidly and may ignore the road rules occasionally.

High-risk driver (score between 76 and 100)

You love the thrill of driving and are likely to take risks to raise your adrenaline levels, such as cornering at high speeds and accelerating rapidly. You enjoy creating an element of risk and you feel alive when you can experience the freedom of the open road at speed. Your thrill-seeking tendencies increase the chances of you being involved in a collision.

Think about your driving, especially when you have a near miss. There may be situations that make you feel excited and enjoy taking risks, especially on open country roads with bends and hills where you may feel like putting your foot down and cornering at speed. Remember that severe crashes are more likely to happen on rural roads.

Find out more about driving on country roads at this website.

https://think.gov.uk/road-safety-laws/#country-roads

And watch these videos.

https://think.gov.uk/campaigns/?filters=.country-roads

Next steps

- Reflect on how your personality affects the way you drive. Do you have a tendency to try to impress others with your driving or gain excitement through driving?
- Remember that accelerating rapidly may mean that other road users are unable to predict what you're going to do next. Try to remain aware of this and drive defensively.
- Resisting the urge to speed can make driving more enjoyable and give you a greater sense of control.
- Consider whether you drive differently when driving alone or with particular types of passenger. Try to recognise this tendency and take steps to drive safely no matter who is (or is not) in the car with you.
- Think about the consequences of being involved in a crash and the effects it would have on your friends and family.
- Recognise the triggers that make you drive in a way that increases your risk of being involved in an incident. Are you more likely to take risks when you're under time pressure? Are you more likely to take risks when you're annoyed or tired?

Stress, mood and emotions

The association between stress and involvement in road traffic incidents is well established. Studies have found that people who have experienced recent traumatic life events (for example, divorce) have a greater risk of crash involvement.

There are thought to be 2 main reasons for this link

- Drivers who are stressed may be distracted by thoughts about their personal problems.
- Stress may cause drivers to lack the necessary motivation to avoid hazardous driving situations.

> It has been estimated that drivers who have experienced stressful events such as personal conflicts, illness, bereavement or financial difficulties are 5 times as likely to cause fatal crashes as drivers who have not been subjected to such stressful events.

People react to stress in different ways. Some drivers may experience high levels of stress even in routine driving conditions, whereas others remain calm and untroubled during the most difficult traffic environments and situations.

Remember

If you have anxiety or depressive illness that affects your memory or concentration, disturbs your behaviour or gives you suicidal thoughts, you should seek medical advice before driving. You might also need to notify the Driver and Vehicle Licensing Agency.

Road layout and driver stress

The road layout itself is an important aspect of the environment that can affect the way you drive. For example, junctions with poor visibility are dangerous because of the difficulty of hazard detection, but you may reduce your personal safety and the safety of other drivers if you overreact by worrying excessively about the problem.

On the other hand, feeling some risk while driving may help to reduce the likelihood that you'll become overconfident and underestimate your chances of being involved in an incident. It may also help you to develop safe coping strategies such as looking carefully before you emerge from a junction.

Self-reflection

What kind of road layout do you find most difficult? For example, roundabouts, rural roads, motorways, etc.

Consider the link between road layout and your personality when driving. For example, do you put your foot down and enjoy the feelings of speed and exhilaration when you're confronted with an apparently empty road?

Are there certain kinds of road layout that trigger a reaction in you?

Time pressure

Driving under time pressure often leads to high-risk behaviour such as speeding and dangerous overtaking. This is particularly true for people who drive for work or those who have a busy schedule. The pressure may be due to your employer imposing strict deadlines or it may be a perceived time pressure that you place on yourself.

Not being able to reach a destination by a certain time only creates a problem if missing that time leads to some kind of penalty. In many situations there's no particular punishment for being late, apart from inconvenience, and you can remove the perceived pressure by calling ahead from a safe place with the engine switched off.

Self-reflection
Heavy traffic earlier on your journey means you're late for an important appointment or to make a delivery.

Ask yourself
- Are the few minutes you might save really worth the risks you're tempted to take by driving too fast?
- What are the true consequences of lateness? Will being late really affect your employer's business?
- Can you pull over and call ahead to let the customer know you're running late due to heavy traffic?
- Would your employer or customer really want you to increase the risk of an incident and its consequences for yourself, other road users and the vehicle?

Improving your coping strategies

When you're driving under time pressure, you may use ineffective coping strategies that not only fail to deal with the stress but also create more risk for you and other road users.

A better coping strategy would be to
- plan your journey in advance
- give yourself as much time as possible by leaving early
- avoid travelling at busy times whenever you possibly can
- recognise how the stress of being under time pressure might affect your driving
- take some slow, deep breaths. Deep, controlled breathing stimulates the parasympathetic nervous system – the part of your nervous system that helps you to relax.

Other good coping strategies include

- being extra-vigilant when you know you're feeling stressed. Switch your attention from thinking about the source of stress to concentrating on the driving task
- focusing entirely on your driving. After all, arriving at your destination unharmed is the most important thing.

Self-reflection
Think about how your driving differs when you're under time pressure.

Do you often find yourself running late and wishing you'd organised things better?

Are you more likely to take risks when you're running late?

Self-reflection scenario
You're driving on a country road on the way to visit a friend. You're running a little late and try to make up time by driving faster.

Ask yourself

- What's going through your mind? Are you thinking more about the consequences of being late than the consequences of having a crash?
- Have you taken into account the dangers of driving too fast on country roads?
- How much time are you really likely to save by driving a few miles an hour over the speed limit?
- Will it really matter if you're a few minutes late?

Strategies for safer driving

- Remember that you have ultimate control over how you choose to drive.
- Try not to create additional pressure by worrying about being late. Remember that the only pressure is the pressure you place on yourself.
- Pull over in a safe place, switch the engine off and phone your friend to let them know you're going to be a little late.
- Take it easy and enjoy the drive. You'll then arrive feeling relaxed and happy to see your friend, rather than stressed and irritated.

Angry driving

Angry drivers frequently express their irritation by behaving aggressively towards other road users. This can include

- verbal abuse
- gestures
- flashing lights
- tailgating
- horn blowing
- lane hogging.

Not surprisingly, such behaviour is known to be dangerous. Angry drivers may spend less time assessing situations and are quicker to allocate blame to others.

> **Anger while driving is linked to negative views about other road users and often leads to intimidation tactics. These include behaviours such as tailgating, risky overtaking or trying to teach other road users a lesson.**

Moods and angry driving

Your mood can change quickly in response to

- what's going on in your life
- traffic situations
- other road users.

Driving in a bad mood

- changes your driving style
- impairs driving performance
- increases your risk.

Angry driving impairs hazard perception

It's important to realise how much influence a bad mood can have on your ability to detect and respond to hazards. To be a safe driver, you need to be able to 'search' the road environment for developing situations. Feelings of frustration, anger or impatience may lead to a failure to detect developing hazards in your peripheral vision and may lead you to spend more time looking at certain hazards than responding to others. This is because strong emotions such as anger tend to take up a lot of your brain's processing capacity, leaving less for you to concentrate on your driving.

Self-reflection scenario

You're driving in the city at rush hour when someone pulls out right in front of you and you have to brake sharply. You're very annoyed and use your horn. You shout at the driver, who looks quite nervous and holds up their hand to apologise. You then accelerate sharply around the driver and continue on your way. You can feel the tension in your body.

Ask yourself

- What was going through your mind? Did you think that the driver deliberately pulled out in front of you?
- What if the driver was distracted and made a mistake? Would that change how you reacted?
- Have **you** ever made a mistake while driving?
- Does getting annoyed help the situation or change anything for the better?
- How did your reaction increase your risk?

Strategies for safer driving

- Try to give other drivers the benefit of the doubt. Remember that in most cases they do not deliberately set out to annoy you.
- Recognise that getting annoyed will only make the situation worse, by putting you at risk.
- Reframe the incident in a more positive way: instead of focusing on the other person's error, take pride in the way you were able to react to the hazard and avoid a collision.
- Choose to change the way you think about other road users who make a mistake. After all, we all make mistakes sometimes.

Test yourself

Driving these days is stressful, and all drivers get frustrated or angry in traffic from time to time. Think about how angry each of the following traffic situations would typically make you feel.

	Not at all angry	A little angry	Fairly angry	Very angry	Extremely angry
Someone in front of you does not move off straight away when the traffic lights turn green					
Someone is driving too fast for the road conditions					
A pedestrian walks slowly across the middle of the street, slowing you down					
Someone is driving too slowly in the outside lane and holding up traffic					
Someone is driving very close to your rear bumper					
Someone is weaving in and out of the traffic					

	Not at all angry	A little angry	Fairly angry	Very angry	Extremely angry
Someone cuts in right in front of you on the motorway					
Someone cuts in and takes the parking spot you've been waiting for					
Someone fails to indicate before turning off					
Someone is driving more slowly than is reasonable for the traffic flow					
A slow vehicle on a winding road will not pull over and let people pass					
You see a police car watching traffic from a hidden position					

	Not at all angry	A little angry	Fairly angry	Very angry	Extremely angry
Someone backs out right in front of you without looking					
Someone goes through a red light or 'stop' sign					
Someone beeps their horn at you about your driving					
Someone coming towards you does not dip their headlights at night					
At night, someone drives right behind you with their headlights on full beam					
You spot a speed camera site ahead					

Section one | The human factors in driving

	Not at all angry	A little angry	Fairly angry	Very angry	Extremely angry
Someone is slow to park and holds up traffic					
Someone speeds up as you try to pass them					
You're stuck in a traffic jam					
Someone pulls out right in front of you when there's no-one behind you					
Someone makes an obscene gesture towards you about your driving					
Someone is driving well above the speed limit					
Someone shouts at you about your driving					

	Not at all angry	A little angry	Fairly angry	Very angry	Extremely angry
A cyclist is riding in the middle of the lane, slowing down the traffic					
A police officer pulls you over					

Self-reflection

Reflect on the driving situations that make you lose your temper and ask yourself what you can do to reduce your stress levels. Finding different strategies to tackle frustrations in traffic often makes you feel more in control and less prone to angry outbursts.

For example, it's highly unlikely that the driver in front of you who keeps braking sharply is deliberately trying to provoke you; they may just be lost. Remember that you have the power to change the way you think about this situation. Understanding your own triggers for outbursts is the first step towards controlling your feelings and increasing your tolerance of other road users and traffic situations.

Summary

In this section, you've

- learned about the limitations on our mental capacity to process information
- looked at the way your thoughts and feelings affect your driving decisions
- considered how your level of confidence in your abilities influences the way you drive
- reflected on your personality characteristics and discovered whether you're a thrill-seeking driver
- learned how angry and stressed driving can compromise your safety.

As you can see, no single human factor predicts risky driving. Risky driving is likely to involve a complex set of circumstances and interactions between several different elements

1. your perceived level of risk, driving abilities, stress, mood, fatigue, personality, etc
2. your personal experiences as a driver: how long ago you passed your driving test, the amount of training you've received, your driving record, etc
3. situational factors: having passengers in the car, the purpose of the journey, etc
4. your chances of being caught and punished for committing a driving offence on your journey
5. non-human factors that will determine the level of risk for individual journeys, such as
   - the objective level of risk – for example the casualty rates on the road you're driving on
   - other factors you cannot necessarily control, such as the time of day or the weather.

How can you drive better?

- Use the self-reflection exercise below before you drive.
- Make sure that you're aware of your cognitive and emotional state before, during and after your journey.
- Outside of work time, driving is usually an activity you can do at your own pace. You have a large amount of control over several elements that directly influence the way you drive; for example
    - when to begin your journey
    - what vehicle to use
    - which roads to take.

Self-reflection

Before you start driving, ask yourself the following questions. If the answer to any of them is 'yes', do not drive until you're safe to do so.

- Are you angry, stressed or upset about anything? Might this impair your ability to drive defensively?
- Are you in a bad mood? Are you distracted by things that are going on in your life?
- Are you under time pressure?

Section two

📱 Other influences on your driving

In this section, you'll learn about

- what to do about distractions while you're driving
- how fatigue increases your risk of an incident
- the dangers of driving after using alcohol or drugs
- how technology can influence your driving behaviour
- new developments in the road environment.

Distractions

In-car entertainment systems, mobile phones, satellite navigation (sat nav) systems and passengers all have the potential to divert your attention away from the road and increase your risk. This is known as 'distracted driving' and it's a major cause of road traffic incidents. It's important to know how to avoid distractions – or cope with ones you cannot avoid – and stay focused on the road.

Facts
A recent study found that 80% of road traffic incidents involved some form of driver inattention within the 3 seconds before the incident occurred.

Mobile phones

You **MUST NOT** use a hand-held mobile phone or other similar device when driving, except to call 999 or 112 in a genuine emergency when it's unsafe or impractical to stop.

If you hold and use a phone while driving, you could get a fine of up to £1,000, 6 points on your licence, and a driving ban.

You can use a phone with hands-free access, as long as you do not hold it at any time. However, your ability to remain focused on the road could still be reduced: it's the mental distraction that increases your risk, not just the physical element of holding a handset.

If you're involved in a collision while using a hands-free device, you may still be open to prosecution for not being in proper control of your vehicle, or even for dangerous or careless driving.

The growth of mobile phone technology has given rise to a type of distraction that did not exist until comparatively recently. An increasing number of drivers may be tempted to use social media, take photos or videos, scroll through playlists or play games.

Extensive research, from both the UK and abroad, shows that people who use a mobile phone while driving are 4 times more likely to be involved in a crash than people who do not use their phone while driving. The level of impairment caused by using a mobile phone is actually more severe than driving with a blood alcohol concentration of 0.08% (the current legal limit in the UK). This is mostly due to the mental distraction and divided attention that's caused by the phone conversation. Irrespective of whether the device is hand-held or hands-free, drivers using a mobile phone

- are much less aware of what's happening on the road around them
- are more likely to miss road signs
- are not able to maintain proper lane position and a consistent speed
- are more likely to tailgate
- react more slowly and take longer to brake
- are more likely to enter unsafe gaps in traffic
- feel more stressed and frustrated.

Facts
- You're 4 times more likely to crash when using a mobile phone while driving – and 23 times more likely to crash while texting.
- Taking your eyes off the road to access social media or to check or send email or messages impairs your ability to respond to hazards.
- Even an ignored call can impair driving ability.
- Using a mobile phone at the wheel means your reaction times slow by about 30%, making you more dangerous than someone who's driving while over the drink-drive limit.

Find out more about the dangers of using a mobile while you're driving by watching this video.

think.gov.uk/campaign/mobiles-2022

Tip
- Turn your mobile phone off while you're driving and let your incoming calls go to voicemail.
- If you need to use your phone as a sat nav, you should secure it in a cradle or on a windscreen mount. It must not block your view of the road and traffic ahead.
- Wait until you're safely parked before making a phone call, sending a text or checking social media.
- The person on the other end of a mobile phone call will not know that your attention is being diverted away from driving unless you tell them.
- If your passenger tries to show you pictures, videos or messages on their mobile phone while you're driving, ask them not to. Tell them you'll look when you've stopped driving.

Self-reflection
Have you ever had a near miss when using the phone while driving?

Other sources of distraction

Satellite navigation systems

Sat nav systems offer a wide variety of features to aid navigation. They're integrated into some vehicles and are also available as portable devices that you attach to the windscreen or dashboard. As they present both audio and visual information, they can cause breaks in concentration that draw the attention of the driver away from the road.

Tip
- Program your sat nav before you start your journey.
- Select the route you prefer and think about traffic congestion and times of day. This can help you to avoid delays and save fuel.
- Position your sat nav so that it does not obstruct your vision but you can still glance at it easily when necessary.
- Make sure that your sat nav does not obstruct an airbag.

- Stay alert to road signs, as you would if you were not using the sat nav.
- Do not rely on your sat nav alone, as you may have set the destination incorrectly. You should also make sure that the maps in your sat nav are up to date before you plan your journey.

In-car entertainment systems

Many people use in-car entertainment systems to listen to music or watch DVDs. These systems can be a major source of distraction for drivers because

- adjusting radios, CD players or MP3 players diverts your attention away from the road
- sound from passengers' DVD, laptop or tablet devices can affect your concentration.

Some drivers believe that music helps them to stay awake. However, one of the major disadvantages from a safety perspective is that fine-tuning radio controls and scrolling through playlists means that your attention is diverted from driving to adjusting the device.

You should **never** use DVD players or personal computers while you're driving.

Tip

- Set up a car playlist so that you do not need to adjust your music while you're driving. Make sure it's long enough for your journey.
- Pre-set your radio controls before you set off. Changing them on the move could be dangerously distracting.
- Keep the volume at a reasonable level. Loud music can reduce your ability to notice or react to hazards.
- In particular, make sure your music is not so loud that you cannot hear warning sounds from your vehicle or external warnings (horns and emergency sirens).
- Be careful not to get too 'drawn in' to the music in your car. This, too, can distract you from what's happening outside and affect your ability to respond to hazards.
- Be aware of the type of music you listen to while driving. In general, research suggests that up-tempo beats can cause you to increase your acceleration and take more risks, while slower-paced music may improve your driving behaviour.

Passengers

Passengers can also be distracting – especially for young and novice drivers. Responsible passengers will observe you as you drive and adapt their conversation and behaviour accordingly.

If you find that passengers are distracting your attention from your driving, either
- stop the vehicle in a car park, lay-by or service area and continue your conversation there, or
- tell them that your concentration is being affected.

Children

Children can be a major source of distraction, particularly if they're tired, hungry or bored by the journey.

In a study of journeys with rear-seat child occupants, children accounted for 12% of all potential sources of driver distraction. Over 75% of parent drivers were found to be turning around or using the rear-view mirror to look at their children, 16% engaged in conversation and a further 7% assisted their children by passing food and drink, etc. Drivers with children in the car were also significantly more likely to have their eyes off the forward roadway for more than 2 seconds while the vehicle was in motion.

- Try to keep children entertained by packing snacks, drinks and games along with you, so their attention is focused on something else. However, do not give the goodies out as you're driving; either stop somewhere safe or put them in a place where the children can easily access them without distracting you from the road.
- Consider playing them films or TV shows on mobile devices. Just be mindful of the sound level, in case it affects your concentration.
- If you're on a long journey, make sure you schedule regular comfort and exercise breaks.

Food and drink

Eating at the wheel can lead to a loss of concentration and often means you have only partial control of your vehicle.

- If you're going on a long journey, make sure you eat before you leave.
- Schedule regular stops to eat, drink and go to the toilet.
- Drink plenty of water to avoid dehydration, as this can negatively affect your concentration.
- Stop in a safe place before you take a drink.

Distracted driving and the law

In the UK, courts have the authority to decide whether **any** distraction (not just a mobile phone call) was a key contributory factor in a collision and made the driver negligent in their responsibility towards other road users. The introduction of new laws on causing death by careless and inconsiderate driving has opened the door for drivers to be prosecuted and potentially imprisoned for any form of distracted driving that results in a fatality.

Self-reflection scenario

You're driving a long way and are keeping yourself entertained by listening to some music. You do not want to listen to some of the tracks and keep skipping to find the ones you like. Now you decide to change the artist you're listening to and start scrolling through the list to find the one you want.

Ask yourself

- What could you do to make sure you stay focused on your driving?
- Is there anything you could do before you set off to minimise the risk of being distracted?

Strategies for safer driving

- Decide before your journey starts what kind of music you want to listen to.
- Set up your in-car entertainment system in advance to minimise your levels of distraction.
- Choose a reasonable volume level and make sure you can hear internal and external warning sounds.
- If you need to change your music, pull over in a safe place to do so.

Fatigue

In this section, we deal with feeling tired, sleepy or lacking in energy, or 'zoning out'; for example, on a long, boring stretch of road.

People tend to think of driver fatigue as something that's only experienced by long-haul lorry drivers and others who regularly spend long hours in a vehicle, but it affects us all.

Driver fatigue – the facts

Your driving performance can be affected by factors such as

- the time of day you're driving
- how long you've been awake before you start driving
- how long you spend driving on a particular journey
- the road environment.

Being a drowsy driver means you're

- three times as likely to be involved in a collision or near miss
- at risk of being involved in the 16% of all collisions (more than 20% on motorways) that happen as a result of sleepiness.

Remember

- Your body is naturally tired between the hours of 2 am and 7 am, and between 2 pm and 4 pm, with major peaks in risk at 3 am and 3 pm. Your chances of having a fatigue-related crash increase by 6 times when driving between the hours of midnight and 6 am.
- If you drive after being awake for 18 hours, your driving is comparable to that of a drunk driver.
- Your fatigue-related risk strongly increases when you've been driving for more than 2 hours.
- Fatigue sets in more quickly on some roads than on others. Motorways, for example, tend to be monotonous, with little visual stimulation to keep you alert. Roads such as these tend to make you feel tired.

How does fatigue affect your driving performance?

When you're fatigued, it
- affects your ability to scan for hazards
- impairs your judgement of speed
- makes it harder for you to maintain a straight path.

It can also have an impact on your reaction time; if a hazard unfolds suddenly, you're poorly equipped to react and avoid a collision.

It's not clear whether this kind of impairment is due to a driver being so tired that they lack the motivation to drive safely, or whether they fail to monitor their driving performance as they grow more tired.

The effects of fatigue can strike quickly, particularly among drivers with underlying health issues or lifestyle factors that increase their likelihood of becoming fatigued. Many medications can increase drowsiness. Additionally, health problems such as sleep apnoea can cause fatigue. Sleep apnoea is when, during sleep, your breathing stops for short periods of time, affecting the quality of your sleep. This can lead to 'microsleeps' during the day, or when you're supposed to be awake. A microsleep is when you actually fall asleep for a moment, often without even realising it. As with mobile phone use, fatigue can be used to determine driver negligence in the event of an incident, and it can result in a criminal conviction.

Self-reflection
If you're tired before you start your journey, or become fatigued during a long drive, how does it affect your driving? Are your reactions slower? Do you tend to use your mirrors less? Do you drift out of your lane and become more erratic in your speed choices?

How can you reduce your risk of a fatigue-related crash?

The increase in risk brought about by driving when you're tired means that it's vital to make sure you're well rested before a long journey. You should also plan regular rest breaks.

Stop and rest

When you're tired, the quality of your driving can degrade to such an extent that the only way to deal with it is to stop as soon as it's safe and legal to do so. If you're on a motorway, pull in at the nearest service area or leave at the next junction. The only time you're allowed to stop on the hard shoulder or in an emergency area is in an emergency, so you **MUST NOT** stop there to rest.

If it's not possible to stop immediately, open a window for fresh air. Then stop as soon as it's safe and legal to do so.

Self-reflection
What do you do to reduce your fatigue while driving? How can you plan your journey to include breaks and maintain your alertness?

Tip
- Get enough sleep before driving, especially if it's a long trip.
- Share the driving with someone else if you can.
- Travel at times when you're normally awake.
- Stop driving if you become sleepy.
- Stay overnight in a hotel rather than drive while tired.
- Schedule a break of at least 15 minutes every 2 hours.
- Avoid working all day and then driving a long distance.
- Find a safe place to take a short nap.
- Travel with a passenger who's awake and alert.

Alcohol and drugs

Drink-driving

Since the breathalyser laws were introduced in 1967, there have been constant efforts to reinforce the message about the risks of drink-driving. These campaigns have largely been successful. However, while the number of alcohol-related crashes and drink-drive convictions has reduced, it remains a problem. The total number of casualties for drink-drive accidents was 8,700 in 2018. There has been an overall reduction in drink-drive fatalities in the last few decades, but this is mainly attributable to improvements in car and road safety. The most important factor is still the state of the driver.

Facts

The drink-drive limit specified in law for England, Wales and Northern Ireland is

- 35 microgrammes of alcohol per 100 millilitres of breath
- 80 milligrammes of alcohol per 100 millilitres of blood
- 107 milligrammes of alcohol per 100 millilitres of urine.

In Scotland the law is different

- 22 microgrammes of alcohol per 100 millilitres of breath
- 50 milligrammes of alcohol per 100 millilitres of blood
- 67 milligrammes of alcohol per 100 millilitres of urine.

It's a criminal offence to fail to provide a specimen for analysis when required to do so by a police officer.

Self-reflection

What plans do you make before drinking alcohol to ensure you do not drive while over the limit? Do you know how long the alcohol will stay in your system? Have you ever taken a chance, hoping you will not get caught?

The best approach is not to drink any alcohol at all before driving. Many drivers find themselves on the wrong side of the law the 'morning after', not realising that they're still over the limit as a result of the previous evening's alcohol consumption. If in doubt, do not take the chance – your driving may still be impaired and you could cause a collision.

The police conduct breath tests on all drivers at the scene of an incident, so even if a collision was not your fault, you would still be breathalysed and, if found to be over the drink-drive limit, prosecuted for drink-driving.

It's not just about 'units'

People are affected differently by alcohol, and each person can be affected differently at different times, so it's important not to assume that the legal limit is equivalent to a certain amount of an alcoholic drink.

The factors that influence the extent to which alcohol affects you, and therefore your driving performance, include
- physical structure – gender, weight and metabolic rate
- food consumption – drinking on an empty stomach means that alcohol is absorbed more quickly
- illness – the dehydration that's associated with many common illnesses increases the rate of alcohol absorption
- medication – some drugs interact with alcohol, resulting in additional effects.

Tip
- Be aware that you could be impaired or even still over the legal limit many hours after your last drink, even the 'morning after'.
- Sleep, coffee and cold showers **will not** help you to sober up. The alcohol is still in your blood.
- Alcohol can make you feel overconfident about your driving. Make sure you fully acknowledge your impairment and ask someone else to drive.
- Agree on a designated driver before you start drinking.
- Save the number of a taxi firm to your phone so you can call for a cab if you need one.
- Find out about public transport routes and times before you go out.
- Do not accept a lift from a driver you know has drunk alcohol.

Drug-driving

The drink-driving laws have been in place for a long time, but more recently there has been a focus on the issue of driving while under the influence of drugs. Given the number of illegal substances that are available, the processes and laws are not as clear-cut as those relating to alcohol. Field impairment assessment (FIA) has been introduced to allow police officers to assess drivers' general impairment and its impact on their fitness to drive.

FIA includes examining your eyes to see how dilated your pupils are, and a series of activities that would be difficult when impaired, such as standing on one leg or keeping your balance with your eyes closed. If you fail an FIA, you'll be arrested and taken to a police station to have further tests – usually a blood test to detect the presence of specific substances.

The police can also use 'drugalysers' to test you for cannabis and cocaine at the roadside.

It's illegal to drive if either

- you're unfit to do so because you've taken legal or illegal drugs, or
- you have more than specified levels of certain drugs in your blood (even if they have not affected your driving).

The law does not cover Northern Ireland but it is still illegal to drive whilst unfit through drugs and you could still be arrested if you're unfit to drive.

If you're convicted of drug-driving, you'll get

- a minimum 12-month driving ban
- an unlimited fine
- up to 6 months in prison
- a criminal record.

Your driver record at the Driving and Vehicle Licensing Agency (DVLA) will also show that you've been convicted of drug-driving. This will stay on your record for 11 years.

For more information about the drug-driving laws, visit **www.gov.uk/drug-driving-law**

For more information about your driving record, visit **www.gov.uk/view-driving-licence**

You can find out more about the effects of drug-driving by watching this THINK! road safety video.

https://think.gov.uk/campaign/more-reason-to-be-paranoid/

Illegal vs legal drugs

We tend to think of drug-driving just in terms of illegal drugs, but many prescription drugs and over-the-counter medicines can have equally detrimental effects on driving performance. To help deal with this problem, the drug-driving laws have been amended. It's now illegal to drive in England, Wales and Scotland with legal drugs in your body if they impair your driving. It's also an offence to drive if you have over the specified limits of certain drugs in your blood and you have not been prescribed them. In Northern Ireland, the law does not distinguish between illegal drugs and drugs that are prescribed or bought over the counter.

Legal highs

The issue of 'legal highs' hits the headlines from time to time, as manufacturers can now provide substances that are not prohibited by current laws but which mimic the effects of illegal drugs. Taking these substances can significantly increase your risk while driving. You could be prosecuted for impaired driving in the same way as if you were using illegal or prescription drugs.

Prescription drugs

Talk to your doctor about whether you should drive if you've been prescribed any of the following drugs

- clonazepam
- diazepam
- flunitrazepam
- lorazepam
- methadone
- morphine or opiate- and opioid-based drugs
- oxazepam
- temazepam.

You can drive after taking these drugs if

- you've been prescribed them and followed advice on how to take them from a healthcare professional
- you're fit to drive to drive even if you're above the specified limits.

It may be helpful to keep evidence of your prescription with you in case you're stopped by the police. Never drive if you've taken more than the prescribed dose.

 Find out more about drug-driving on the THINK! website.

https://think.gov.uk/campaign/breathalyser-for-drugs/

Some medication leaflets and packaging state 'Do not operate heavy machinery'. A vehicle is a piece of heavy machinery, but it's such an integral part of day-to-day life that people tend not to view it as such. It's important to understand that the impaired driving is the illegal act, regardless of the legality of the drug or its source.

Self-reflection

Do you check leaflets and avoid driving as recommended when taking medication?

Do you ask your doctor or pharmacist for advice about driving and taking medication?

Can you nominate a driver to help you to get around if you're taking medication?

- If in doubt about the effects medicines might be having on your driving ability, do not drive until you have all the information you need.
- Do not stop taking your medicines, prescribed or otherwise, but do talk to your doctor or ask your pharmacist for information.

 To find out which health conditions or medical treatments you may need to tell DVLA about, visit this website.

www.gov.uk/driving-medical-conditions

75

New technologies

Electric vehicles

Electric vehicles (EVs) have a part to play in solving the problem of CO_2 emissions. However, their public health and environmental impact is dependent on how they're driven. For example, EVs are heavier and more responsive than equivalent internal combustion engine vehicles. This means that

- the amount of dangerous particulates released into the air by tyre and road wear is higher
- the momentum contributed by an EV to any collision is greater.

As an EV driver, there's even more reason to accelerate and brake gradually and take care to control your speed.

Compared to traditional combustion engines, EVs produce virtually no noise. This makes it more difficult for pedestrians (especially those who are blind or partially sighted), cyclists and other road users to be aware of them. It's important that you keep scanning for hazards, drive at an appropriate speed and give vulnerable road users as much space as possible.

Since July 2019, all manufacturers have installed an acoustic sound system to their new types of quiet electric and hybrid electric vehicles. When vehicles are reversing or driving at less than 12 mph, sound generators produce a noise similar to that made by a conventional engine. You should make sure that the system is turned on and the sound is working on your vehicle.

Safety strategies for EV drivers

- Make sure that vulnerable road users know you're there by checking whether they've seen you.
- Slow down if you think road users may not know that you're there. Use your horn, if necessary, taking care not to startle others.
- Allow other road users plenty of time and space if you're not sure whether they're aware of your presence.

You should also

- plan your journeys to include charging sessions
- keep your EV warning sounds switched on to alert pedestrians to your vehicle
- take care to accelerate gradually
- check and maintain your tyres more regularly.

Remember, most EVs are equipped with regenerative braking. This slows your car down without using the brakes. It's useful when you're going downhill because it helps to recover energy lost during acceleration, which also helps to extend your vehicle's range.

Vehicle engineering

Vehicle engineering has seen significant advances in the past 30 years, with the introduction of improved safety measures such as

- inertia-reel seat belts
- airbags
- child seat fixing points (ISOFIX bars)
- anti-lock braking systems (ABS)
- electronic stability control (ESC)
- independent vehicle safety testing – European New Car Assessment Programme (Euro NCAP).

Vehicle manufacturers have also invested heavily in the research and development of technology that

- helps you to avoid a collision
- protects the occupants of a vehicle as much as possible in the event of a collision.

See the next section on advanced driver assistance systems (ADAS).

Self-reflection

Remember your first car. How different was the interior of that vehicle from your present vehicle? How have you adapted to changes in the vehicles you've driven over the years?

The rise of advanced driver assistance systems

Driving is a complex task in which you need to process lots of information and do several things at the same time. Advanced driver assistance systems (ADAS) help you by taking on some elements of the driving task. For example, they can increase the space between vehicles, and they may react faster in dangerous situations than you can. They improve road safety when used properly, and they can make doing a lot of driving less demanding and tiring.

As people grow older, or when they develop disabilities, more automated help with driving can be useful. However, ADAS should **never** be seen as a substitute for the driver, who must always pay attention to the driving task. Assistance features and self-driving vehicles are not the same thing. ADAS do not make a vehicle self-driving at any time.

It's important to understand your vehicle's assistive features, and the benefits and risks of each one. It's equally important to learn how to adapt to driving vehicles fitted with ADAS.

Forms of ADAS
- Adaptive cruise control (ACC) can automatically adjust your speed and separation distance to maintain enough space between you and the vehicle in front. This is designed to help you and minimise risks.
- Another form of ADAS combines ACC, lane centring and speed sign recognition to allow you to take your hands off the steering wheel for a short time but not your eyes off the road. You must remain engaged with the driving task and must monitor the environment at all times.

The development of ADAS

Driver assistance systems have a long history that began with anti-lock braking systems (ABS) in the 1970s.

By 2020, ADAS were installed in about 10% of the one billion cars in use around the world. They're increasingly available as standard or as an option in mainstream cars – even entry-level models. For example, lane-keeping assist (which provides steering assistance to keep a vehicle in its lane) was installed in over half of new cars sold in Europe in the first half of 2021.

While the number of vehicles fitted with ADAS is growing, it'll be several decades before the technology appears in all vehicles. Millions of older cars will remain on the road for a long time. Despite this, it's projected that the overall market share for vehicles with some level of automation will increase to approximately 40% of vehicle travel by 2040.

How ADAS work

To assist in the driving task, ADAS use sensors and cameras to
- detect obstacles and driver errors
- check for driver alertness.

Warnings are sent to help you to avoid collisions with vehicles or pedestrians that are approaching your blind spots. ADAS can also help you with things like parking and lane keeping. Other functions can keep your vehicle a set distance from the one in front and control your speed. ADAS can even bring your vehicle to a complete stop in an emergency.

Here are some examples of ADAS.

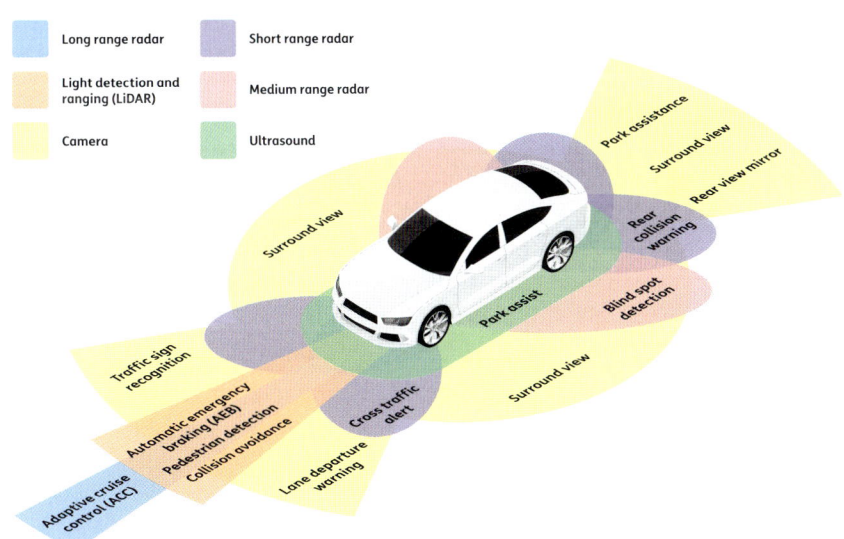

 Remember
It's essential to know where the sensors are on your vehicle and how to keep them in good working order. Your vehicle's manual will provide the details.

Vehicle engineering and behavioural adaptation

Sometimes, improvements in vehicle safety can have a negative effect on the way that people drive. A notable example is ABS, technology designed to help drivers stop efficiently.

A project called the Munich taxi driver study looked at the behavioural impact of the introduction of ABS. Researchers studied collision rates and observed the driving behaviour of taxi drivers with and without ABS fitted in their cabs. They found there was no significant difference in their collision rates – in fact, the rate for drivers of ABS-equipped vehicles was slightly higher than the rate for those without ABS.

Human responses to technology are not always straightforward. The Munich study revealed that the drivers with ABS-equipped vehicles
- braked harder
- cornered more sharply
- left less space in front of them
- failed to maintain lane positioning
- failed to merge with other traffic in a safe manner.

This was likely to be due to the drivers **feeling** safer and therefore taking more risks.

Remember
ADAS cannot protect you if you become complacent and take more risks.

Self-reflection
Have you noticed whether the technology in your vehicle has led to a change in the way you drive? Do you feel safer and therefore take more risks? Do you drive differently in new or hired vehicles that you know have state-of-the-art safety systems and gadgets?

Self-reflection scenario

For the past 3 weeks, you've been driving a new company car that has cruise control. You really like being able to keep to a fixed speed so that you can take your foot off the accelerator and let the car drive at the speed you've selected. It's been particularly useful on long, boring motorway journeys.

However, on your last motorway journey, you suddenly had to brake sharply to stop your car crashing into the back of a line of stationary traffic, which had stopped for roadworks up ahead. This was the first time in ages that you'd had to stop so quickly to avoid a collision and you wonder whether the technology has had an impact on your driving.

Ask yourself

- How can you make sure that you stay focused on the primary task of driving, even when using in-vehicle technology?
- What can you do to make sure your ability to respond to hazards is just as sharp when you're using in-vehicle technology?

Strategies for safer driving

- Technology is there to reduce your workload to help you to drive safely. Be aware that when workload levels are really low, your attention might start to drift.
- Stay alert when using new technology by consciously maintaining control of the vehicle, in the same way as you would when driving without the technology.
- Make sure that you do not rely on technology to get you out of trouble. Ultimately, you must be in control of the vehicle.
- Do not be tempted to drive at higher speeds than normal because of in-vehicle technology.
- Driving at a fixed speed is inappropriate in many traffic situations. Assess the traffic regularly and cancel cruise control in good time.
- Keep scanning the road ahead and checking your mirrors to look for hazards when using cruise control.

Positive and negative effects

Sometimes in-car technology can have both positive **and** negative effects on driver safety.

Positive

Sat-nav systems can help you to find your way around and avoid the worry and distraction caused by getting lost. They're particularly useful in challenging situations, such as complex junctions, or when unexpected diversions or road conditions make signs more difficult to follow. This means that you can concentrate on monitoring the constantly changing traffic situation for hazards, and making safe decisions, rather than focusing on finding the correct route.

Similarly, ADAS are designed to make driving much safer. When sensors are on, they have the advantage over your eyes and ears as they can scan in every relevant direction at once. The reaction times (for example, when the sensors detect a hazard) are much shorter than a human driver can manage too. When switched on and used appropriately in the right conditions, sensors can reduce collisions and injuries. They might even save your life, those of your passengers and other road users around you.

Self-reflection

Does your vehicle have collision-avoidance systems?

If so, are you sure you know how to use them correctly?

Seven of the most common new technologies are
- forward collision warning
- automatic emergency braking
- lane-departure warning
- lane-keeping assist
- adaptive headlights
- blind-spot detection – do you fully understand how to work it?
- intelligent speed assist (ISA).

Negative

It's easy to become over-reliant on in-car technology and leave it to make too many of the decisions. Most of us will have heard the stories about people who followed the directions on their sat navs, only to find themselves travelling the wrong way down one-way streets or driving down railway lines! In these situations, the drivers may have become 'passive' and placed too much trust in the navigation system, rather than actively observing road signs or planning their journeys in advance. This means that something that's meant to help is often given a much higher level of control than may be safe.

Self-reflection

How can you make sure that you always stay focused on your driving – allowing the technology to support you, rather than allowing it to take control?

How can you make sure that you're prepared for potential hazards and changing circumstances?

The challenge of responding to changes in technology

Drivers will face different challenges as assistive and automated vehicle technology grows and changes. The technologies work differently from car to car. For example, the way that adaptive cruise control (ACC) works in one vehicle may be different from the way it works in another – even if both vehicles are the same make and model. Driver mistakes when using assistive and automated technologies suggest that developers of these systems are still learning how to take human limitations into account fully.

Another problem is that motor manufacturers use very similar names for features that vary widely in their function. This can be confusing.

For example, most manufacturers set their ACC so that using the accelerator will temporarily increase the speed above the one set. When you release the accelerator, the ACC resumes speed control. However, on some vehicles, the ACC is set to standby mode after you have exceeded the set speed for more than one minute. When this happens, you must actively resume ACC operation if required.

It's crucial that you read the vehicle's manual before using ADAS features and that you fully understand their limitations (see more information on page 79). Relying on 'trial and error' learning during ADAS operation is dangerous.

Any dealer or hire company should explain which ADAS features a vehicle has, and exactly how you should use them to keep you safer. The government, the Society of Motor Manufacturers and Traders and representatives of related industries have all agreed that they should do this for you. If they do not offer this advice, it's important to ask for it.

Tip
- A wide variety of ADAS are available in cars these days. Make sure that you read your vehicle's manual to fully understand how they work before they take you by surprise while driving.
- Do not rely on technology to let you know about an imminent collision. Stay focused and in control of the vehicle at all times and let the ADAS assist you instead.

Adapting to ADAS

Overall, the research shows that ADAS are good for road safety. But we also know that the less drivers need to do, the more likely they are to lose concentration and become drowsy, inattentive or distracted. While ADAS reduce drivers' workloads, you need to make sure you avoid

- over-reliance on technology
- distraction
- boredom
- 'zoning out' and failing to monitor the surroundings carefully.

Be aware of the risk that you may come to rely on the system even when you're told that it's not safe to do so. For example, you might expect that it'll respond to all the critical information necessary for safe driving. Too much trust in the systems may mean that you

- stop concentrating on your driving
- fail to monitor the traffic
- are not prepared to react when the system reaches its limits.

Here are some of the ways you need to make a conscious effort to adapt when you use an ADAS feature for the first time, or after using it for a while.

Anti-lock braking system
- Take care to maintain your following distance.
- Resist the urge to brake more harshly.

Adaptive cruise control
- Do not choose a higher speed setting than you'd normally drive at.
- Take care to maintain your following distance.
- Remain alert and responsive to critical events.

Lane-keeping assist
- Do not over-rely on warnings to maintain lane position.
- Keep a straight course and do not drift across the lane, trusting that the car will not leave it.

Reversing aid
- Keep up your direct glances behind, and your shoulder and mirror checks.

To find out more about some ADAS, have a look at the following AutoNinja videos made by Co-Pilot

- lane keep assist: **youtu.be/5FxsklTSwdY**
- lane departure warning: **youtu.be/NHzO-TD8OMc**
- electronic stability programme: **youtu.be/5s9RgA1gRsw**
- brake assist: **youtu.be/nRuoX6hvxKU**
- auto emergency braking: **youtu.be/EUMOowbBr0I**
- adaptive cruise control: **youtu.be/3mT4x7DzHO0**
- tyre pressure monitoring system: **youtu.be/I_bFvhijtd0**
- traffic sign recognition: **youtu.be/w5yqfO3TjJQ**
- rear cross traffic alert: **youtu.be/VENFb2Q845g**
- parking assist: **youtu.be/N_wOcVjK5tU**
- intelligent speed assist: **youtu.be/eDahK-Mp8HY**
- high beam assist: **youtu.be/ZFcI4ercIjw**
- forward collision warning: **youtu.be/s88NVRQM60A**
- ECall: **youtu.be/S3m-e4GbR90**
- drowsiness detection: **youtu.be/OLkwL_spN0M**
- blind spot warning: **youtu.be/nt1DJ8tiO9g**
- around view cameras: **youtu.be/mibuXiQL_k8**
- anti-lock brakes: **youtu.be/CvQBNUBHOVA**

The road environment

The UK road network has been engineered to work efficiently with the vehicles it carries and to give drivers as much information as possible to help them make safe decisions. Road engineering has also provided a physical environment that's designed to minimise the risk of serious injury or death when incidents do happen. See the safe system approach on page 125.

Innovations in road engineering through the years have included

- traffic lights
- roundabouts
- consistent warning signs
- effective and widespread safety barriers
- street lighting
- improvements to visibility at dangerous junctions
- wider roads
- converting crossroads into mini-roundabouts or intersections with signals
- traffic-calming measures in residential areas.

However, some researchers believe that driver behaviour adapts to changes in road engineering in the same way as it adapts to changes in vehicle engineering. In other words, as was found in the Munich taxi driver study, when drivers feel safer, some of them will take more risks. When roads have been widened, for example, some drivers have chosen to increase their speed because they think the road is safer.

 ### Self-reflection
Have you noticed whether your driving changes when you're on a well-engineered road? Think about a newly built road you've driven on, with fresh tarmac and no potholes. Or perhaps it's a widened road with clearer road signs. Do you feel that these roads are safer and therefore drive differently?

Engineering for behaviour

More recently, we've seen local innovations such as 'shared space' (also known as 'naked roads') in parts of the UK.

Shared space is a kind of street design that has
- minimal road markings
- few signs.

The theory is that reducing or removing the usual markings encourages road users to look around and decide who should have priority of movement.

Self-reflection
Have you ever found yourself in a shared-space zone?

How have you made your way through unmarked or unsigned areas and taken the needs of other road users into equal consideration?

Summary

In this section, you've
- considered the effects of distractions and fatigue on road safety
- looked in more detail at impaired driving and seen how alcohol and drugs can affect your driving ability
- learned how developments in vehicle technology and the road environment can affect your behaviour as a driver.

The road environment is constantly changing. Technological developments, engineering initiatives and new laws all have an influence on the way we drive. Our roads are safer than they've ever been, but you can help to make them even safer by understanding your own driving behaviour and the way you interact with your vehicle and the road.

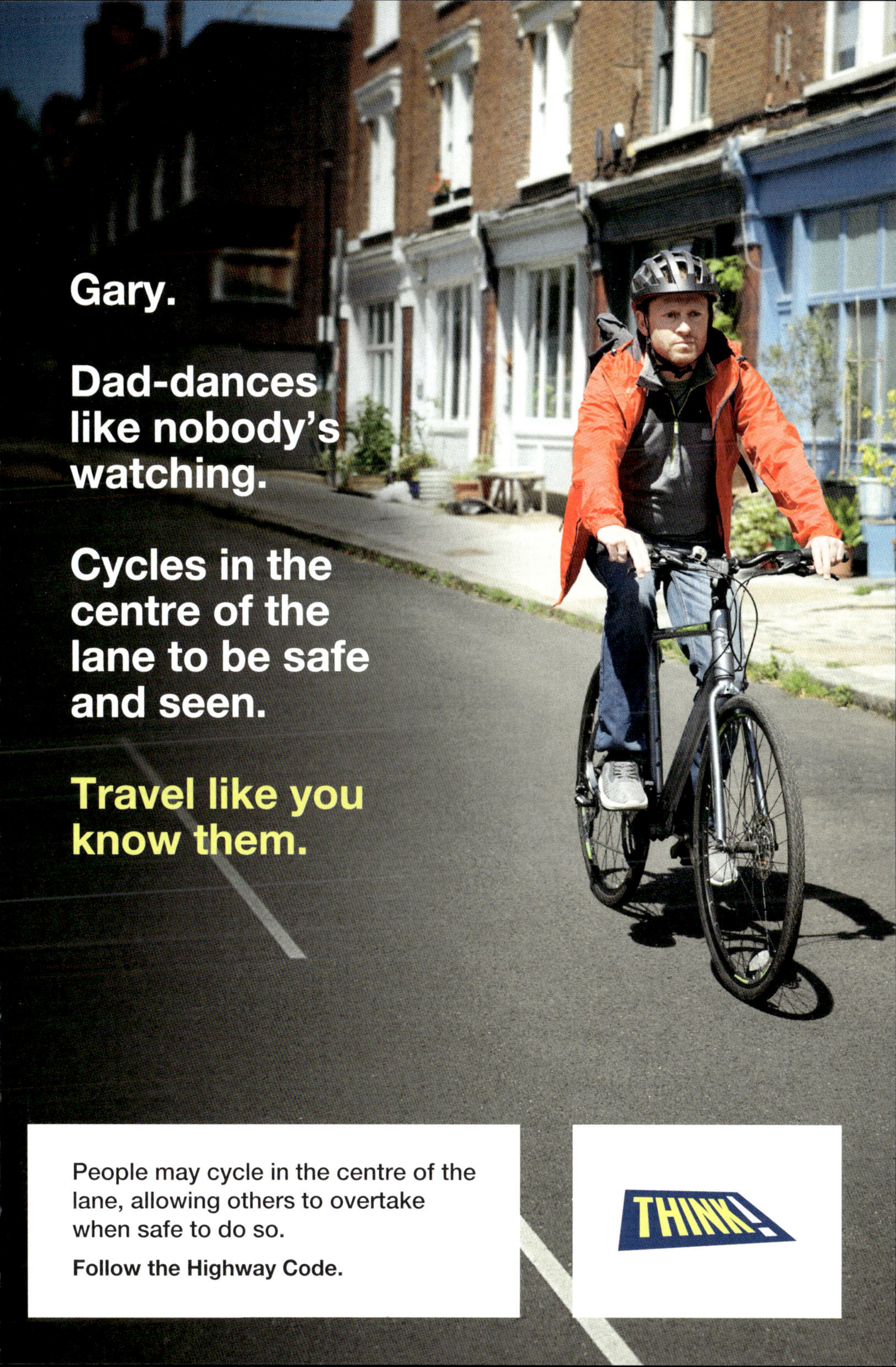
Gary.
Dad-dances like nobody's watching.
Cycles in the centre of the lane to be safe and seen.
Travel like you know them.
People may cycle in the centre of the lane, allowing others to overtake when safe to do so.
Follow the Highway Code.
THINK!

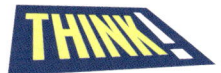

Section three

Developing better strategies

In this section, you'll learn about

- anxiety and driver ability
- some general tips for a less stressful drive
- how to deal with challenging driving scenarios
- learning to drive and managing anxiety
- strategies to help you stay on the right side of the law
- ways to adjust and reassess your driving as you get older
- how to improve your reaction to stressful situations.

Feeling nervous about driving

You might think that feeling nervous about driving is something that only happens to you, but you'd be wrong. Many drivers experience situations that make them feel anxious, nervous or confused. This could lead them to avoid certain journeys or, in extreme cases, any kind of driving activity at all. It goes without saying that neither of these outcomes is desirable. In both scenarios, a lack of confidence can affect your enjoyment of the social and professional opportunities that a vehicle can provide.

There are many reasons why you might feel nervous about driving. For example

- You may have learned to drive a long time ago but not driven for the past few years. You may not have the confidence to return to driving after such a long gap.
- You may put too much pressure on yourself to be a perfect driver and worry about the mistakes you might make.
- You may have recently been involved in a road traffic collision or near-miss, or been convicted of a traffic offence, and are now questioning your driving abilities.
- You may be going through a particularly stressful time in your life, such as changes to your financial or domestic situation, and this may be affecting how you feel. These feelings can be a serious distraction when driving.
- You may have lost confidence in your driving because someone has criticised you.
- You may have recently passed your driving test and feel that your skills are not sufficient to cope with certain situations.
- You may feel there are too many demands on you as a driver. Perhaps you're noticing the effects of ageing, such as slower reaction times. Or perhaps you have a medical and/or physical condition – such as diabetes or arthritis – that's affecting your confidence in driving.
- You may have recently become a parent for the first time. The extra responsibility this brings may have caused you to become nervous about driving with the baby in the car.

If any of these sound familiar, then this section will give you a number of tools and techniques to help you enjoy your driving life again. Whatever the reasons for a decline in your self-belief, you'll be able to overcome your concerns and return to driving with confidence.

Which scenarios make you feel nervous?

Some drivers are anxious about particular types of road or road features, such as motorways, roundabouts or junctions. Others are anxious about particular traffic situations, such as

- when other vehicles, particularly heavy goods vehicles, are driving too close behind them
- driving in congested urban conditions or during the rush hour
- driving at night or in bad weather.

Self-reflection
What makes you most nervous when you're driving?

How does being nervous affect your driving?

You may worry that the demands of driving are greater than your ability to cope with them. That's where effective coping strategies can help.

 Buy The Official DVSA Guide to Winter Driving e-learning short course to help you drive safely in winter.

safedrivingforlife.info/shop/the-official-dvsa-guide-to-winter-driving

Anxiety and driving ability

Feeling anxious about driving has a negative effect on your driving performance, and makes you more likely to make a mistake. This is because you become distracted, worrying about what **might** happen instead of focusing on what you actually need to do. Reducing your anxiety levels will help you to concentrate on your driving, and therefore you'll be more likely to enjoy the experience.

Stress: brain, body and mind

When you feel anxious, physiological changes take place in your brain and body. These changes can have a big effect on your driving.

In normal, relatively mild fear reactions, such as those experienced by a nervous motorist, key neurons throughout the brain fire more rapidly, sending information around the brain and body, and creating a general state of anxiety. Perspiration levels, breathing rates and muscle tension increase. Being anxious can have a negative effect on your ability to process information about hazards and can increase your chances of missing important information. When you make a mistake or do something wrong, this heightens your state of anxiety, worry or fear. With repeated experiences over the long term, there may even be a downward spiral that leads you to give up driving altogether.

The kind of personality we have can determine how we respond to stress. The good news is that you can develop the characteristics of individuals who cope better with stress by using the strategies covered in this section. Such 'hardy' individuals believe that they can influence events and have control over their lives. They take responsibility for their own actions and respond flexibly to challenges as they arise. Hardy individuals view challenges as a normal part of everyday life and see them as an opportunity for growth and development. They're more likely to welcome challenges and not see them as a threat or try to avoid them.

General strategies for a less stressful drive

The following strategies will help you to stay safe, feel less stressed and get more enjoyment from your driving.

- Choose a route that places fewer demands on you, such as a road you're familiar with.
- Allow more time for your journey.
- Avoid driving at busy times (where possible).
- Avoid driving in bad weather.
- Focus on the task of driving. If you're distracted by worries or concerns, you should find a safe place to stop and only carry on driving when you can do so safely. Try not to let your worries or concerns about driving affect your concentration.
- Avoid being distracted by your mobile phone. Switch it off before you start driving.
- Reduce your mental workload by reducing your speed. The faster you drive, the more information you need to process.
- Find a quiet place to practise manoeuvres that might cause you stress, such as three-point turns in tight streets or parallel parking.
- Find an approved driving instructor (ADI) and ask for some additional training to top up your driving skills.

Coping with challenging scenarios

Have a look at the following scenarios and think about how you usually approach the situations they describe. Once you've read through them, take a look at the coping strategies underneath each one. How do they differ from your normal approach?

Use the scenarios in this section to develop your self-reflection toolkit: think about additional scenarios that are particularly relevant to you. Go through the steps to develop your self-awareness and the strategies you'll need to improve your driving.

Junctions

You're about to emerge from a junction and are feeling worried about the volume of traffic on the main road. You've been waiting a little while for a safe gap in the traffic and now there's a queue of vehicles behind you. You're starting to feel anxious about holding up the traffic. You think 'I must try and move out soon'.

You look in the rear-view mirror and the driver behind you is very close; you're afraid they might start sounding their horn to get you to move out when you're not ready. You can feel your anxiety levels rising.

Ask yourself
- How can you stay calm when you think other road users may be getting frustrated with you?
- What can you do to make sure you make safe decisions even under pressure?

Strategies for safer driving
- Remember that **you** are in charge of your vehicle and the decisions you make. Other road users must not influence you. Do not let yourself be intimidated into taking risks.
- Remind yourself that having to wait for a safe gap is due to the busy traffic and is no reflection on your driving skills. It may take time to judge the speed of the traffic, but this is a critical part of knowing when it's safe to go.
- Do not be distracted by what the drivers behind you might be thinking. You cannot know what's going on in their minds. Concentrate on making a sensible assessment of the situation in front of you.
- If your view to the left or right is obstructed, you'll need to take some action to improve it, such as slowly edging forward.
- Remind yourself that there will eventually be a safe gap in the traffic. You will not be at this junction forever. Only go when you feel it's safe.
- Let other drivers deal with their own situation while you deal with your situation. They should be able to understand how busy the traffic is when it's their turn.

Roundabouts

You feel worried about pulling out on to a roundabout and being in the correct lane to exit. Sometimes you wait a long time to pull out. Other vehicles come round the roundabout so fast and they do not always indicate to let you know whether they're continuing round or turning off. Sometimes it feels like they're coming from all directions.

Ask yourself

- How can you approach a roundabout without feeling overwhelmed?
- What can you do to cope better with the demands of using roundabouts?

Strategies for safer driving

- Take some lessons with an ADI and get additional practice at driving on roundabouts. Practice makes perfect.
- Tell yourself that you can do this. After all, you've done it many times before.
- Take slow, deep breaths if you feel your anxiety levels rising.
- Check the road signs as you approach the roundabout. Plan how you need to approach, enter, drive around and exit the roundabout. Your plan will vary according to the design of the roundabout and your destination, but it should allow you to deal with the task safely.
- If you're on a spiral roundabout, remember that the lines spiral outwards from the centre of the roundabout and each lane has a designated exit. Road markings are used to keep vehicles in the correct lane, and to guide them towards the appropriate exit. You should comply with any signs, traffic lights and lane markings, and indicate only to change lanes as part of the normal mirror–signal–manoeuvre routine (see Rule 133 of The Highway Code). You can find out more about spiral roundabouts in 'The Official DVSA Guide to Driving – the essential skills'.

How to use a roundabout

Going left
- Indicate left as you approach.
- Approach in the left-hand lane.
- Keep to that lane on the roundabout.
- Maintain a left turn signal throughout the roundabout.

Going ahead
- No signal is necessary on approach.
- Approach in the left-hand lane. If you cannot use the left-hand lane (because, for example, it's blocked), use the lane next to it.
- Keep to the selected lane on the roundabout.
- Check your mirror, especially the nearside exterior mirror.
- Indicate left after you've passed the exit just before the one you intend to take.

Going right or full-circle
- Indicate right as you approach.
- Approach in the right-hand lane.
- Keep to that lane and maintain the signal on the roundabout.
- Check your mirrors, especially the nearside exterior mirror.
- Indicate left after you've passed the exit just before the one you intend to take.

Remember

If there's a problem when you get to your exit on a roundabout, do not worry. You can usually go all the way round, so – if you can do so safely – keep going and focus on your exit when you reach it again.

Driving in unfamiliar locations

Your familiarity with a route can affect the way that you drive. A routine trip on familiar roads may not worry you, but a longer trip on unfamiliar roads might present more of a challenge.

If new experiences make you nervous, some practice at dealing with these kinds of situations will help. Improving your skills through extra professional lessons and revisiting The Highway Code can improve your confidence, making driving a far more pleasurable experience for you.

Remember
- Anxiety can be reduced if you're well prepared for the journey.
- You can cope with difficult situations by taking control.

Long journeys

You want to visit family members who live quite a distance away from you, but you have not driven such a long way for ages. The only option is for you to make the journey by car, but you've never driven this route before.

You wonder whether you have the ability to drive all that way. Fast traffic makes you feel anxious, and the more you think about the journey and what might happen, the more nervous you become. You think to yourself 'What if something happens? What if I get lost? What if I cannot cope with the traffic?'

Ask yourself
- How can you better plan your journey so that you know where to go on unfamiliar roads?
- What can you do to reduce your anxiety about going on a long journey?

Strategies for safer driving

- Contact an ADI and get some additional practice at driving on unfamiliar roads.
- Use your previous driving experience. You probably have many memories of driving safely on different kinds of roads and this will help you to cope in unfamiliar locations – even though you may not have encountered these particular roads before.
- Asking an experienced driver to accompany you on the journey might be reassuring, provided they encourage you and do not become a distraction.
- Perform basic maintenance checks on your vehicle before you leave. Check the
  - oil level
  - engine coolant level
  - tyre pressure
  - lights and indicators
  - screen-wash level.

- Take emergency supplies. These should include blankets, a basic first-aid kit, a warning triangle and water.
- Make sure your mobile phone is fully charged in case of emergencies.
- Use a route planner on the internet and print out the details of your journey. Study them before you travel.
- Check the traffic news for hold-ups or roadworks.
- Identify an alternative route that you could use if required.
- Take a map with you. Sat nav devices can be very useful, but it's good to have a back-up in case the technology lets you down.
- Always program your sat nav before setting off.
- Avoid driving at busy times of day.
- Avoid congested routes.
- Drive during the day and in good weather if possible.
- Allow plenty of time for your journey and schedule regular rest breaks.
- You might want to reduce the demands on you as a driver by using cruise control, but make sure that you stay alert and do not become over-reliant on the system.
- Being anxious will make it more difficult to drive safely. Try to put your worries out of your mind and concentrate on your driving instead.

Driving with children

You pick your son up from play school. You strap him safely into his child seat in the back of the car. After 10 minutes of driving in busy town traffic, he asks for a drink. When you tell him he can have a drink when you get home, he starts to cry. You turn around and try to comfort him but the cries get louder. You're approaching a complicated junction and need all your concentration.

Ask yourself

- How can you better prepare for driving with your child?
- What can you do to minimise the chances of your child being a distraction while you're driving?

Strategies for safer driving

- Avoid turning around in your seat to check on your child, as this will take your attention away from the road.
- Avoid looking in the rear-view mirror at your child too often, as you need to concentrate on the road.
- Tell yourself that your child is safely strapped in and there's no need for concern. You'll soon be home.
- As soon as they're old enough to understand, start teaching your child about how they can help you to be a safer driver by being quiet.
- To reduce the chances that your child will complain about being hungry, give them a healthy snack before you set off.
- Play their favourite audio book or songs.
- On long trips, take regular breaks and make sure children have something to keep them amused – a few books, a tablet, an in-car DVD player or some favourite small toys.
- Make getting there part of the fun – for example, watching out for a familiar landmark (such as a church spire) that means they're nearly home.

Remember
If there's an emergency, pull over in a safe place before you help your child.

Driving at night

You need to make a trip after dark, but you're worried that the glare from vehicle headlights might dazzle you. You're concerned about your ability to see hazards properly and even about getting lost in the dark. You remember how difficult it is to manoeuvre your car into the tight spot in the car park. It will be even more difficult at night.

Ask yourself

- What can you do before driving at night to make sure you're as safe as possible?
- Once you're on the road, what can you do to maximise your safety?

Strategies for safer driving
- Certain types of glasses may be unsuitable for night driving, so check with your optician.
- Check the operation of the front and rear lights, brake lights and indicators, including hazard lights, before you set off.
- Use road markings and cat's eyes to help you see the direction of the road ahead.
- The lights of vehicles ahead can help you see where there's a bend and when you need to reduce your speed.
- Only overtake other vehicles when you can see that it's safe to do so.

Dealing with dazzle

- Keep your speed down when you leave brightly lit areas, to allow time for your eyes to adjust.
- Leave a large enough gap between your vehicle and the one in front, so that your lights do not dazzle the other driver.
- Adjust your dashboard lights to a comfortable level, as they can cause reflections.
- If you're dazzled, slow down or stop in a safe place until your vision returns to normal. This should only take a moment.
- Use dipped headlights where there are other vehicles, to avoid dazzling their drivers.
- Do not be tempted to flash your headlights at drivers who are using full beam. It's better to encourage others to be courteous drivers by being courteous yourself.
- If you feel your anxiety levels rising, stop your vehicle in the nearest lay-by or other suitable place and take slow, deep breaths. This activates your body's relaxation response.

Driving in wet weather

It's a Friday night and you're driving home after a hard week at work. The traffic is heavy and stormy weather conditions are making this a very difficult journey. You think other people are driving too fast and you're feeling out of your depth.

Ask yourself

- Are you accurately assessing the risk of driving in the rain? Do the wet road and spray from other vehicles mean that your ability to drive safely is affected?
- What's going through your mind? Is your desire to get home and out of the rain making you more anxious?

Strategies for safer driving

- Remind yourself that you've driven in these kinds of conditions many times before and always returned home safely.
- Use dipped headlights so that other drivers can see you.
- Keep your speed down. Windscreen wipers struggle to cope with very heavy rain, so your view of the road ahead will not be as good as it could be. Driving at a lower speed will give you more time to react to hazards that are not immediately visible through the rain.
- Make sure that you keep the windscreen free of smears and streaks and always keep your washer bottle topped up.
- Wet weather reduces your tyres' grip on the road. Allow at least double the separation distance between you and the vehicle in front.
- If things are getting too much for you, pull over in a safe place and wait for the traffic to die down. It will be much easier to continue your drive when the roads are quieter.
- While you're waiting, do something different to help yourself relax. For example, buy a cup of coffee and read a newspaper. Enjoy some time to yourself.

Driving in snow and ice

It's been snowing and you have to make an essential journey. There are a couple of inches of snow on the roads and with every car that passes, slush is thrown up onto your car. The slush is turning to ice around the edges of your windscreen.

Suddenly you feel your tyres lose grip as you take a corner and slide a little towards the centre of the road. Around the bend, your wheels hit a rut in the snow and you find it difficult to steer. You start to feel worried about driving in these conditions.

Ask yourself

- How can you drive more safely in snow and ice?
- What can you do to minimise your risk when driving in slippery conditions?

Strategies for safer driving

- Firstly, consider whether your journey is really necessary. Can you cancel your arrangements and drive when the roads are safer?
- If you must drive in snow and ice, make sure you keep your speed down.
- Controlling a skid can be very difficult, so drive gently to avoid getting into one in the first place. Choose as high a gear as possible and avoid harsh use of the steering, brakes or accelerator.
- Be especially careful on corners and bends, where there's a greater risk of your tyres losing grip – particularly if you're driving too fast.
- Increase your following distance in icy conditions. Remember that the stopping distance in these conditions can be ten times as long as it would be in good driving conditions.
- Regularly check that your tyres have a good depth of tread and are inflated to the right pressure. Any shortcomings will be more apparent in slippery conditions.
- Make sure you have plenty of winter screen wash in your windscreen-washer bottle before you start driving.
- Remain vigilant for hazards that occur in snow and ice. Other road users may be struggling. This is especially true of large vehicles, whose wide tyres do not grip well on snow and ice.
- Be aware that there may be potholes under the snow and slush.

Parking

You're on a busy high street and are looking for somewhere to park. You spot a place and indicate to alert other road users that you're pulling into the space. As you slow down and drive past the space so that you can reverse in, it becomes clear that the space is not as big as you thought it was.

You position your car and start reversing. The parking sensors come on and you start to feel anxious as you realise that you're not in the right position to get into the space safely. It means that the waiting traffic will have to wait even longer.

Ask yourself

- How can you prepare yourself to carry out a safe parking manoeuvre in this situation?
- What can you do to control your feelings of anxiety about parking?

Strategies for safer driving

- It's not a good idea to rely solely on parking sensors; always use your own observation skills.
- Look in all directions continuously when reversing. Use your mirrors and turn around in your seat to look out of the windows.
- Moving slowly allows you greater control in a small space. If you move the vehicle slowly and steer quickly, you can manoeuvre the vehicle more effectively. Once you start turning into the space, coordinate your controls to keep the vehicle moving at a slow speed.
- Do not worry about holding up other road users. Focus on safely executing the parking manoeuvre.
- Remember that everyone makes mistakes sometimes.
- Do not underestimate the value of allowing extra time for finding a space and parking.
- If you feel you need to develop your parking skills, practise on your own on a quiet street or contact an ADI.

Driving near motorcyclists and cyclists

You approach a junction and look for a safe gap in the traffic on the main road before you pull out. You see a gap coming up in the traffic to the left and quickly check the traffic to the right. You're about to emerge, when at the last second, you slam on your brakes. A motorcyclist is right in front of you and you did not see her at all. Another second and you would have knocked her over.

Ask yourself

- How can you make sure you spot vulnerable road users in good time?
- What do you need to bear in mind when emerging from a junction?

Strategies for safer driving

- Make sure you fully observe the traffic, in both directions. The commonest cause of a collision with a motorcyclist or cyclist is when the driver fails to look properly. This may be because riders are smaller and therefore more difficult to see, or because there are fewer of them in traffic and you're not expecting them.
- Remember that you cannot accurately judge the speed or distance of oncoming motorcyclists and cyclists unless you look at them for long enough. This may be several seconds.
- Look well into the distance to spot motorcyclists, who may be difficult to see.
- Be aware that motorcyclists and cyclists may look at you, but this is not the same as them expecting you to emerge from the junction. Just because you've made eye contact with them does not mean it's safe to emerge.
- To make a safe decision about whether to emerge, you need to fully realise what you're looking at. Some drivers 'look but fail to see' oncoming motorcycles and make a decision to pull out on the basis of what seems to be an empty road.
- Cyclists can sometimes be in your blind spot at junctions, so make sure you take good all-round observation before turning.
- Allow cyclists plenty of space before you turn.

Learner drivers and managing anxiety

Learner drivers experience anxiety for several reasons. For example, they

- could worry about understanding new vehicle technology and how it works
- could worry about getting manoeuvres wrong
- might have had a bad experience as a passenger
- could feel stressed about learning a new practical driving skill with a driving instructor
- might worry about using specific roads (for example, busy roads, complicated roundabouts and so on)
- might already feel anxious about other things going on in their lives.

If you're planning to learn to drive, accept that you might feel anxious and that's OK. Try not to get frustrated if you make a mistake or are struggling to learn. Driving is a skill that takes time to develop.

Sometimes, people put off driving lessons because they're worried about them, but this can create a bigger problem. Avoiding lessons can reinforce worry and increase your anxiety levels. Taking small steps towards your driving goals, while being supported by your driving instructor, is the best way to overcome feeling anxious.

Remember
Learners are not expected to drive perfectly; even the best drivers were learners once.

Self-reflection

Today is the day of your first driving lesson. You felt OK when you got up but now you're feeling anxious and overwhelmed.

Remind yourself that

- anxiety is a normal human emotion that many people experience
- it's OK to feel anxious when learning to drive
- a good driving instructor will be supportive and patient with you and make sure that you learn at your own pace.

It's also important to recognise that putting additional pressure on yourself can be a source of anxiety. For example, if you need to pass your test to get a job, it can make you feel stressed and hold you back.

The truth is that learning to drive takes practice and there are no shortcuts. The more pressure you put on yourself to get a licence quickly, the more difficult it becomes. The key is to focus on developing your skills at a speed that suits you and gives you the best possible chance of becoming a safe, competent driver.

Strategies for safe driving practice

Building up your skills gradually will help you to tackle anxiety and consolidate your skills more effectively. For example

- Develop your skills in bite-sized chunks.
- Focus on the things you did well rather than just thinking about the things you did wrong.
- If you start to feel anxious, tell your instructor that you will need to pull over somewhere safe and settle down for a couple of minutes. When you feel more relaxed, continue with your practice.

If your anxiety becomes overwhelming, there are a range of helpful techniques that you can use to help manage it. For example, classic breathing techniques can help to make you feel more relaxed.

To do this, breath in (inhale) deeply and breath out (exhale) fully. Do not try to count or control your breath, simply carry on taking deep breaths until you feel better.

Remember

If you feel unsafe because anxiety has affected your ability to concentrate, you must tell your instructor and pull over when it's safe to do so.

Remember

Ask your instructor to help you understand the proper use of any assistance or automated features in the car. Familiarising yourself with new technology will help you drive safely, responsibly and efficiently for a lifetime, not just for the practical driving test.

▶ Learner drivers can read more about managing their anxiety on the Ready to Pass? website.

readytopass.campaign.gov.uk/driving-test-nerves

Driving offences

With experience, your ability to anticipate what might happen becomes automatic and less effort is required to process information. While it's good to develop greater confidence in your driving ability, it can have negative effects if you become too relaxed and feel that you can get away with breaking the law.

The most common driving offences include speeding, using a mobile phone while driving, and going through red lights. You may not have thought about doing any of these immediately after passing your driving test, but as time has worn on you may have felt justified in breaking the rules occasionally. Although these offences are not always intended (speeding, for example, may be due to a lapse in concentration), most of the time they're deliberate, conscious actions.

Ask yourself what's at stake if you're caught committing a traffic offence. Which of these aspects are most important to you?

- I want to avoid getting penalty points on my driving licence.
- I want to avoid being fined.
- I want to avoid the effects of a traffic offence on my car insurance premium or my job.
- I want to avoid being involved in a collision.

Think about these consequences the next time you find yourself about to break the rules of the road.

Self-reflection scenario

Driving after a traffic conviction

Think about why you decided to break the law. Was there something different going on that day that made you feel justified in taking a risk? Do you regularly break the rules of the road?

Consider whether your driving style is due to certain habits that you can break, or due to your perception of risk. If you've read the previous sections of this book, you may now have a different understanding of these factors.

Strategies for safer driving

- Be aware that road safety is your first priority.
- Be aware that you have the same chance of being caught as anyone else.
- Think about the potential consequences of your actions.
- Do not get upset or angry about minor things. Accept that other road users get it wrong sometimes.
- Give yourself plenty of time for your journey, so you will not be tempted to drive too fast or jump the traffic lights.
- Never use a mobile phone while driving, even hands-free. It can distract you from the road environment and cause you to miss important information.
- Read road signs carefully and make sure you know what the rules are. If you need to refresh your knowledge, take a look at The Highway Code.
- Make sure you're fit to drive. Never drive if you've taken drugs or if you've been drinking alcohol.
- Do not drive when you're tired. You're not only more likely to commit an offence, but also more likely to be involved in an incident.

Driving as you get older

Many people have an active lifestyle in later life and want to continue to drive in order to maintain their independence. This is to be encouraged, as continuing to drive is associated with healthy ageing and general wellbeing.

Even though older drivers tend to have safer attitudes to driving and commit significantly fewer traffic offences than other age groups, some age-related deterioration in driving ability is inevitable for all of us. Only you know whether the changes in your driving ability are due to the effects of ageing or poor health, or whether you have a lack of confidence that can be improved with the right approach.

Most older drivers tend to give up driving at about the right time. However, some older drivers stop driving prematurely through lack of confidence, and this can have a large impact on their lives. Making your own decision about when to give up driving is much better than being pressured into doing so by others.

Coping strategies for older drivers
- Drive at quieter and less congested times of the day.
- Try to avoid driving at night or in poor weather conditions.
- Give yourself plenty of time for your journey, and plan your route thoroughly before you set off.
- If you're no longer confident about performing certain manoeuvres, try to plan your journey to avoid them. For example, you could avoid taking your car into congested areas by using park-and-ride facilities.
- Make sure your car is serviced regularly.
- Think about whether your car is still suitable for the kind of driving you do. If you have a large car that's difficult to manoeuvre, consider changing to something smaller.
- Are you taking full advantage of modern technology? Automatic gearboxes and more advanced features such as parking assistance can be valuable driving aids.
- Keep yourself physically fit. This will make driving less tiring.
- Exercise your mind by taking part in mentally stimulating activities.
- Ask for feedback on your driving from people you trust, such as family members.

 Some driving instructors offer refresher lessons for older drivers. Find your local driving school on this website.

www.gov.uk/find-driving-schools-and-lessons

Some local authorities also offer help to keep you driving with confidence.

Test yourself

Do you agree or disagree with the following statements? Be honest!

1. I believe I can deal safely with risky situations on the road.
2. If I felt my driving was becoming unsafe, I would change my driving habits.
3. My driving skills are not as good as they used to be.

Might you be biased in your assessment of your driving skills? Are you willing to make some changes to your driving habits? If your driving skills are not as good as they were, follow the advice in this section. If you still feel you're struggling to cope, it might be time to seek medical advice.

Warning signs

According to the National Highway Traffic Safety Administration in the US, the following are signs that it may no longer be safe for you to drive

- forgetfulness
- unusual or excessive agitation
- confusion and disorientation
- loss of coordination and trouble with stiffness in joints
- trouble walking, swallowing or hearing
- dizziness when changing positions; tripping and falling
- shortness of breath and general fatigue
- difficulty following verbal instructions and/or giving inappropriate responses to those instructions.

Additional tips to increase older driver safety

The US-based Center for Disease Control and Prevention offers this advice to older drivers

- Exercise to improve strength and flexibility.
- Ask your doctor or pharmacist to review your medicine, to reduce side effects and interactions.
- Have your eyes checked once a year.
- Drive during the day and in good weather.
- Plan your route before you drive.
- Leave an appropriate distance between yourself and the car in front of you.
- Avoid distractions inside the car.
- Consider alternatives to driving, such as using public transport or riding as a passenger with friends or family.

Improving your reaction to stress

When we rise to a challenge and succeed, we feel better about ourselves. Similarly, if you can overcome your worries and build your confidence in driving, then it will increase your self-esteem as a driver. Everyone can feel anxious, worried and stressed while driving at one time or another. These kinds of reactions can be due to the traffic or road environment as well as what's going on in your life at the time. Quite simply, you'll drive better if you develop good coping strategies to manage the demands of driving.

Think about the following approaches to dealing with driver stress.

Poor approaches

1. Confrontation – you antagonise other drivers by flashing your headlights or using the horn in anger to let them know they were at fault. You tend to want to show other drivers what you think of them.
2. Driving concerns – you have a tendency to be critical of yourself and worry about your shortcomings as a driver. You tend to blame yourself for getting too emotional or upset while driving.
3. Avoidance – your attention span is reduced to avoid dealing with the demands of driving. You may refuse to believe that anything unpleasant is going on and carry on as if nothing had happened.

Good approaches

4. Task focus – you tend to cope with the demands of driving by making a special effort to look out for hazards. You observe, anticipate and act in good time when you meet a difficult traffic situation or encounter bad weather.
5. Reappraisal – you have positive thoughts about your driving and look on the challenges you meet as useful experience. You tend to think about the benefits you gain, such as becoming a more experienced driver.

From the list above, task focus and reappraisal are the most effective strategies and should form the basis of your mental approach to driving. Confrontation and driving concerns are particularly ineffective because they're linked with negative and impaired driving behaviour. For example, confrontation is associated with committing traffic offences and making driving errors, while driving concerns is associated with self-criticism and driving errors.

Remember
You can be a better driver by developing task-focus and reappraisal coping strategies.

Assessing your coping strategies

Ask yourself which of the following strategies you've adopted on recent journeys and assess your general approach to dealing with stress.

Poor strategies

When driving is difficult

1. I relieve my feelings by taking risks or driving fast
2. I try to make other drivers more aware of me by driving close behind them
3. I show other drivers what I think of them
4. I swear at other drivers (aloud or silently)
5. I let other drivers know they're at fault
6. I flash the headlights or use the horn in anger
7. I blame myself for getting too emotional or upset
8. I worry about what I'm going to do next
9. I worry about my shortcomings as a driver.

Good strategies

When driving is difficult

1. I try to gain something worthwhile from the drive
2. I do not let myself become distracted
3. I feel that I'm becoming a more experienced driver
4. I make an effort to stay calm and relaxed
5. I make a special effort to look out for hazards
6. I concentrate hard on what I have to do next
7. I look on the drive as useful experience
8. I think about the benefits I'll get from making the journey
9. I learn from my mistakes.

Do you mostly use good or poor coping strategies? Try to focus on increasing your use of good coping strategies and reduce your use of poor coping strategies.

Summary

In this section, you've

- seen that anxiety has a negative effect on your driving performance but there are ways to reduce your nervousness and improve your confidence
- learned some strategies to help you manage the demands of difficult driving situations
- considered how you can stay safe on the road by focusing on the consequences of your actions
- reflected on the effects of ageing on driving performance, and explored some strategies to reduce your exposure to unnecessary risk and drive for longer
- examined your reaction to stress while driving, and learned better ways of coping with it.

🚥 **10** DEAD SLOW

HORSES ARE UNPREDICTABLE.

Passing horses wide and slow can prevent the death of drivers, riders and horses

1. Slow down to a maximum of 10 mph
2. Be patient; don't sound your horn or rev your engine
3. Pass the horse wide and slow (2 metres, at least a car's width if possible)
4. Drive slowly away

#thinkhorsethink10

The British Horse Society is a Registered Charity Nos. 210504 and SC038516
Credit: Crown Copyright DVSA

The British Horse Society

Section four

Refresh your knowledge

In this section, you'll learn about

- how the UK's road environment has changed over the years
- the hierarchy of road users and their vulnerability
- speed limits and rules of the road
- the procedures to follow when driving on a motorway
- how to keep your vehicle roadworthy
- what to do in the event of an emergency.

The changing road environment

There's a common misconception that Britain's roads are getting more and more dangerous. In fact, the annual number of road deaths has stayed about the same since 2010. In 2018, there were 1,784 reported road deaths in Great Britain. This is despite the fact that there was 4 times as much traffic on the road as there was in 1960. Developments in road engineering, legislative efforts, driver education and changes to licensing procedures have seen the UK maintain its position as one of the safest countries in which to drive.

The driving timeline

The driving test was first introduced in 1935 to help bring down the number of road-related deaths. Take a look at this timeline showing the changes to driving since 1965 and ask yourself what has changed since you passed your test.

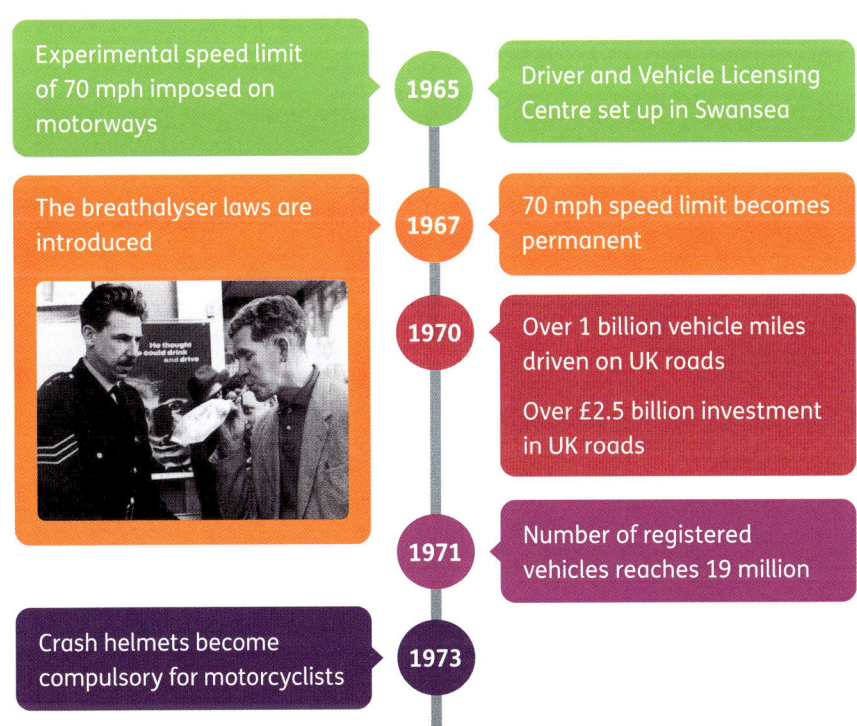

1965
- Experimental speed limit of 70 mph imposed on motorways
- Driver and Vehicle Licensing Centre set up in Swansea

1967
- The breathalyser laws are introduced
- 70 mph speed limit becomes permanent

1970
- Over 1 billion vehicle miles driven on UK roads
- Over £2.5 billion investment in UK roads

1971
- Number of registered vehicles reaches 19 million

1973
- Crash helmets become compulsory for motorcyclists

Timeline

- **1976** — Full driving licences become valid to age 70
- **1978** — The Highway Code introduces the Green Cross Code for pedestrians
- **1981** — Road deaths fall below 6000 per year
- **1983** — Front seat belt law introduced
- **1988** — 'North report' published, leading the way for the introduction of the National Driver Offender Retraining Scheme (NDORS), based on the principle that education rather than punishment may improve driver safety
- **1990** — Over 2 billion vehicle miles driven on UK roads; Over £2 billion investment in UK roads
- **1991** — Fixed speed cameras first appear on UK roads
- **1992** — The police set up NDORS as an option for minor moving traffic offences
- **1996** — Driving theory test introduced; Full rear seat belt law introduced; Road deaths fall below 5000 per year
- **1997** — New drivers automatically disqualified and required to retake the theory and practical tests if they accrue 6 penalty points within the first 2 years after obtaining a full driving licence
- **1998** — Road deaths fall below 3500 per year

2002	Hazard perception test introduced
2003	New law prohibits the use of hand-held mobile phones while driving

2007	Number of registered vehicles reaches 31 million. Road deaths fall below 3000 for the first time since records began in 1926
2010	'Independent driving' element introduced to the driving test: candidates must follow road signs and make their own driving decisions for 10 minutes
2011	770,000 people complete the NDORS speed awareness course

2012	300 billion vehicle miles driven on UK roads
2013	Road deaths reach an all-time low of 1713
2014	Traffic on UK motorways reaches an all-time high of 64.3 billion miles travelled

2015	The driving test is 80 years old
2016	The OECD principles for safe system are published
2017	Changes to the driving test, introducing a longer period of independent driving and use of sat navs

Section four | Refresh your knowledge

2018 — Learner drivers allowed to practise on motorways

Advanced driver assistance systems (ADAS) features are installed in 10% of the 1 billion cars in use around the world — **2020**

2022 — Rules for all types of road users updated in The Highway Code to improve the safety of people walking, cycling and riding horses

The first 'eyes-on, hands-off' ADAS vehicle was approved — **2023** — The number of vehicles in use on UK roads is up to a record 40.7 million (Society of Motor Manufacturers and Traders)

2030 — It's predicted that about 50% of cars in use will include ADAS features

The market share for automated vehicles is expected to increase to 40% of vehicle travel — **2040**

As you can see, the past 50 years have seen major changes to the driving environment and the driver licensing process. Watch DVSA's 'Driving tests: guides for learners' videos and ask yourself how the test has changed since you passed it. Do you think you would still pass today's test? What bad habits have you developed since you gained your licence?

youtube.com/dvsagovuk

The safe system approach

As unsafe actions can never entirely be prevented, road engineers have developed a safe system approach. The system recognises that

- people make errors
- the human body has a limited physical ability to tolerate forces before harm occurs
- improving road safety is a shared responsibility
- all parts of the road transport system must be strengthened, so that if one part fails users are still protected.

Unlike traditional approaches to road safety, the safe system approach acknowledges that a failure of the road traffic system is the cause of many collisions. Roads need to be equipped with a 'forgiving' infrastructure, which considers the vulnerability of human beings.

The safe system is a state-of-the-art approach to traffic safety management. It's recommended to countries worldwide by the United Nations (UN), International Transport Forum (ITF) and the Organisation for Economic Co-operation and Development (OECD).

 Facts

Several countries that used a safe system approach between 1995 and 2000 experienced major reductions in traffic fatalities between 2000 and 2020. For example

Norway: 73% reduction

Sweden: 66% reduction

Safe system pillars

In the safe system model, there are 5 supporting 'pillars' that work together to reduce risk.

Safe roads and roadsides – Roads designed to reduce collision risk and injury severity; for example, safety barriers.

Safe speeds – Speed limits based on collision avoidance and reducing impacts in the event of a collision. This requires speed that is appropriate for the conditions.

Safe vehicles – Designed and regulated to actively prevent collisions (such as vehicles with autonomous emergency braking) or reduce the severity of them (such as vehicles fitted with airbags).

Safe road use – All road users are expected to use the roads safely and be competent, including paying full attention while driving, adapting to the road conditions, not drinking alcohol or taking drugs before driving, not driving when tired and not using a mobile phone.

Post-crash response – The emergency services and the National Health Service (NHS) ensure that road collisions are responded to quickly and investigated.

The hierarchy of road users

An analysis of road fatalities in Great Britain in 2019 found that the type of vehicle most frequently involved in fatal collisions is cars. In contrast, pedestrians and cyclists pose very little risk to other road users but are at the greatest risk of harm if they're involved in a collision.

It's important to check for updates and to refresh your knowledge of The Highway Code regularly at

www.gov.uk/highway-code

You can buy a paperback copy from

safedrivingforlife.info/shop/official-dvsa-highway-code

The Highway Code introduced new rules in 2022 about the hierarchy of road users. The idea is to encourage those who can do the greatest harm to others to reduce the danger they pose. Those at most risk in the event of a collision are at the top of the hierarchy.

The hierarchy
- places the greatest responsibility on drivers of larger vehicles to look out for more vulnerable road users
- promotes safety by encouraging more mutual respect and consideration of other road users.

The Highway Code provides 3 rules to support the hierarchy of road users. These are called the H rules. The H rules consider the safety issues from the perspective of the most vulnerable road users.

Those who cause the greatest harm have the greatest responsibility to reduce the risk they may pose to others

Rule H1

Those in charge of vehicles that can cause the greatest harm have the greatest responsibility to take care and reduce the danger to others. But cyclists and horse riders likewise have a responsibility to reduce the danger to pedestrians. Remember that people you meet on your journey may have impaired sight, hearing or mobility. Their attention might be divided or distracted. It's dangerous to assume that everyone is constantly alert and aware of you.

It's important that all road users remember that they still have a responsibility for their own and other road users' safety. For example, the hierarchy, and Rule H2 in particular, does not mean that pedestrians can neglect their responsibility to follow the Green Cross Code at Rule 7.

Rule H2

All other road users should give way to pedestrians waiting to cross at a junction. Drivers and motorcyclists **MUST** give way to pedestrians on a zebra crossing and to pedestrians and cyclists on a parallel crossing. Drivers and motorcyclists should give way to those waiting to cross. Horse riders should also give way to pedestrians and cyclists on a zebra or parallel crossing. Cyclists should give way to pedestrians on shared-use cycle tracks and horse riders on bridleways. Only pedestrians may use the pavement.

Rule H3

Motorists should not cut across cyclists or horse riders going ahead when turning into or out of a junction. Drivers and riders should not turn at a junction if doing so would cause a cyclist or horse rider to swerve or stop. They should stop and wait for a safe gap in the flow of cyclists, which includes when cyclists are
- moving off from a junction
- passing stationary or slow-moving traffic
- travelling around a roundabout.

Speed limits

In the early part of the 20th century, speed limits were introduced, revised and scrapped on a regular basis. By the time the national motorway speed limit was introduced in 1965, the basic structure of speed limits was established and it remains in place to this day.

You should always keep in mind that the speed limit is the absolute maximum. It does not mean that it's safe to drive at this speed.

National speed limits

National speed limits vary according to the type of vehicle you're driving. Unless road signs say otherwise, the standard national limits are as follows

Type of vehicle	Built-up areas mph (km/h)	Built-up areas, Wales	Single carriage-ways mph (km/h)	Dual carriage-ways mph (km/h)	Motorways mph (km/h)
Cars, motorcycles, car-derived vans and dual-purpose vehicles	30 (48)	20 (32)	60 (96)	70 (112)	70 (112)
Cars, motorcycles, car-derived vans and dual-purpose vehicles when towing caravans or trailers	30 (48)	20 (32)	50 (80)	60 (96)	60 (96)
Motorhomes or motor caravans (not more than 3.05 tonnes maximum unladen weight)	30 (48)	20 (32)	60 (96)	70 (112)	70 (112)

Type of vehicle	Built-up areas mph (km/h)	Built-up areas, Wales	Single carriageways mph (km/h)	Dual carriageways mph (km/h)	Motorways mph (km/h)
Motorhomes or motor caravans (more than 3.05 tonnes maximum unladen weight)	30 (48)	20 (32)	50 (80)	60 (96)	70 (112)
Buses, coaches and minibuses (not more than 12 metres overall length)	30 (48)	20 (32)	50 (80)	60 (96)	70 (112)
Buses, coaches and minibuses (more than 12 metres overall length)	30 (48)	20 (32)	50 (80)	60 (96)	60 (96)
Goods vehicles (not more than 7.5 tonnes maximum laden weight)	30 (48)	20 (32)	50 (80)	60 (96)	70 (112) / 60 (96) if articulated or towing a trailer
Goods vehicles (more than 7.5 tonnes maximum laden weight) in England and Wales	30 (48)	20 (32)	50 (80)	60 (96)	60 (96)
Goods vehicles (more than 7.5 tonnes maximum laden weight) in Scotland	30 (48)	20 (32)	40 (64)	50 (80)	60 (96)

Section four | Refresh your knowledge

Remember
Where no other limit is shown, the national speed limit for cars and motorcycles is
- 60 mph (96 km/h) on a single carriageway
- 70 mph (112 km/h) on a dual carriageway or motorway.

The national speed limit sign

Local speed limits

Local authorities have the power to impose speed restrictions on local roads in areas where the national speed limits are inappropriate. These include

High-risk urban areas	20
High-risk single carriageways	40
Moderate-risk rural single carriageways	50

 You can find more helpful advice in the Department for Transport's 'Know Your Traffic Signs'.

safedrivingforlife.info/shop/know-your-traffic-signs

Variable speed limits

Variable speed limits on motorways are primarily there to smooth traffic flow, reduce congestion and make journeys more reliable. See later in this section for more information.

Appropriate use of speed

Most of us are familiar with the slogan 'speed kills', but it does not reflect the full reality of the relationship between speed and road deaths.

Speed itself does not kill (in fact, fewer incidents happen on motorways) but inappropriate use of speed has great potential to do so. Speeding may not save you any time, either: a 5-mile cross-town journey at an average of 28 mph will take about 10 minutes, while the same journey at 40 mph will only save you a couple of minutes.

 Most of us do not think about the consequences of driving at inappropriate speeds. Watch this video to find out what the consequences could be.

youtube.com/watch?v=0tteHhYh9rU

 Self-reflection

Do you sometimes go over the speed limit?

In what circumstances is this most likely to happen?

What can you do to make sure that you keep to the speed limits?

What were your answers to the last set of questions? If you were honest, you may well have thought of an occasion when you were travelling at an unsafe speed. It's important to realise that speed limits show the maximum speed permitted by law on a particular road. They are not an indication that it's safe to drive at that speed.

Choosing the most appropriate speed involves constant evaluation and decision-making, taking into consideration factors such as
- the type of road – speed limit, quality of surface and engineering features such as speed bumps, narrowing lanes and pedestrian crossings
- the weather conditions – visibility, effect on stopping distance
- the time of day – likelihood of school children, wildlife, farm vehicles, etc on the roads
- the presence and behaviour of other road users.

You should take all of these factors into account to determine the speed at which it's safe to drive.

Remember
Some people think that going over the speed limit by just a small margin is safe, but if you're driving at 35 mph and you hit a pedestrian, you're twice as likely to kill them as you would be if you were driving at 30 mph.

Motorway driving

The UK motorway system has expanded and evolved over the past 50 years and is now a very different place from the early motorways of the 1960s and 1970s. Changes have included variable speed limits, a move away from the standard two- or three-lane format, and increased use of complex junctions and filter-lane systems. To ease congestion, some stretches of the major motorways have been widened to 4 or even 5 lanes, making drivers think more carefully about their lane choices. There has also been a push to combat 'middle-lane hogging', which is now an offence. Traffic patrols target those who obstruct the flow of traffic by occupying an inappropriate lane.

Learner drivers can now practise driving on motorways, as long as they're with an approved driving instructor and in a car fitted with dual controls.

Choosing the right lane

Early motorway guidance referred to the 'slow lane', 'middle lane' and 'fast lane', which encouraged drivers to choose speeds they thought were appropriate for each lane. Unsurprisingly, one person's idea of 'fast' was likely to differ from another person's. The result was that some drivers chose to sit in the 'fast lane' while a growing tailback formed behind them, and other drivers felt provoked to overtake on the inside.

Today, the lanes are referred to as 'lane 1', 'lane 2' and 'lane 3' – and lanes 2 and 3 are described as overtaking lanes – to reinforce the rule that you should stay in the left-hand lane (lane 1) unless you're overtaking a slower vehicle.

Put simply, no vehicle should take a position in lane 2 or above and remain there unless they're approaching or passing a slower vehicle in the lane to the left of them. This gives faster-moving traffic the opportunity to overtake in a controlled manner, which minimises the risk of incidents.

Self-reflection

When you're driving on a motorway, how do you use the lanes? Do you tend to stay in the same lane or do you tend to drive faster than the rest of the traffic and overtake frequently?

Do you use the correct lane(s) when overtaking?

Have you ever remained in an overtaking lane for too long because you were worried that if you returned to lane 1, fast-moving traffic in lane 2 would prevent you from pulling out again?

Changing lanes

The following is general advice when changing lanes on a motorway

- Research has shown that drivers often do not spend enough time assessing potential hazards before pulling out. Make sure that you take your time and always check that it's safe before you make your move.
- It can be frustrating when the roads are busy and you're waiting for a gap in the traffic, but stay calm and relaxed so that you make a safe decision.
- Do not be tempted to take a risk and cause other road users to brake suddenly and move out of your way. They may not react in time and this could have serious consequences.
- Check your mirrors regularly. Make sure you look back far enough to see any fast-moving vehicle, and check carefully for motorcycles.

For more information on driving on motorways, see 'The Official DVSA Guide to Driving – the essential skills'.

 Have you read the most recent advice in The Highway Code about using lanes on motorways? Follow this link to buy the latest edition.

safedrivingforlife.info/shop/official-dvsa-highway-code/

Large vehicles on motorways

If a motorway has more than 2 lanes, heavy vehicles are prohibited from entering the highest-numbered lane (lane 3 on a traditional three-lane motorway), but they're permitted to overtake one another in the other lanes.

Remember that it can be difficult for drivers of heavy goods vehicles (HGVs) to see you, because smaller vehicles can sometimes be hidden in their blind spots. This is especially true of left-hand-drive HGVs, so scanning the road for an indication that they're about to pull out is essential.

You should follow this advice

- Do not speed up when an HGV is passing you. Instead, give the driver room to pass safely, as this will get you out of their blind spot faster.
- If an HGV is signalling to change lanes, give it space. An average HGV travelling at motorway speeds needs an eight-second gap to change lanes.

- If you're alongside or approaching a large vehicle with a view to passing it, and you see its indicator flash, prepare to move out to the next overtaking lane as soon as it's safe to do so.
- HGVs can become unstable in side winds. Keep both hands on the steering wheel when you pass an HGV or when an HGV passes you.

 Remember
Try to avoid sitting alongside any vehicle for an extended period while overtaking.

Controlling traffic on motorways

Some motorways are monitored and controlled by new technological systems, most commonly traffic flow cameras and electronic signs on gantries above the carriageway – one for each lane. This technology helps to reduce congestion and improve journey times.

Motorways that have 3 or more lanes can have variable speed limits shown on overhead signs. These speed limits are shown inside a red circle and are legally enforceable.

On some motorways, the hard shoulder is permanently used as an extra lane. Emergency areas with emergency telephones are provided at least every 2500 metres, in case of an emergency or breakdown, and drivers receive regular information updates via the overhead signs. The signs display information on the current mandatory variable speed limits, as well as indicating whether lanes are closed.

On some sections of motorway, the hard shoulder is used to provide extra capacity during busy periods. The hard shoulder is marked with a solid white line and drivers are only allowed to use it as a running lane when the overhead signs say it's available. If the sign above the hard shoulder displays a red X or is blank, you must only enter it in an emergency, or when told to do so by the police, traffic officers or an emergency sign.

Self-reflection

Have you ever driven on a motorway with traffic management technology?

Do you know what to do if you break down on this type of motorway?

For more information about driving on motorways, see this website.

nationalhighways.co.uk/road-safety/driving-on-motorways/

If you're driving on a motorway and your vehicle develops a problem, you should try to leave at the next exit or pull into a motorway service area. If you cannot leave the motorway, then you should move left onto the hard shoulder or nearest emergency area, where you'll be able to call for help using the roadside telephone. If it's not safe to get out of your vehicle, keep your seat belt and hazard lights on and call 999 immediately.

Vehicle maintenance and breakdowns

You can reduce the chances of your car breaking down with preventive maintenance. Make sure that your vehicle is serviced at the recommended intervals and carry out some simple checks yourself (see below) on a regular basis. Modern cars are very reliable, but being prepared (by joining a breakdown service, for example) and knowing what to do in the event of an emergency will help to increase your confidence in driving.

Is your vehicle ready for your journey?

Just a few checks before you set off, in addition to general vehicle maintenance throughout the year, should make a breakdown unlikely.

Before you use your car, check that

- your fuel tank is full enough for your intended journey. Remember that driving at higher speeds will use more fuel – and there can sometimes be quite a distance between service areas on motorways. Allowing your fuel to run too low can cause running problems and even damage the engine
- the windscreen, windows and mirrors are clean
- all lights (including brake lights and indicators) are working. Replace any dead bulbs immediately. (It's a good idea to carry spare bulbs and fuses.) If you do not feel confident about doing this, your garage should be able to help
- the brakes are working properly. Do not drive with faulty brakes.

Check the following levels before you use the vehicle, following your car manufacturer's advice. Contact your garage if you have any concerns about the

- engine oil
- water in the radiator or expansion tank
- brake fluid
- water in the windscreen and rear-window washer bottles.

Check your tyres and make sure they're legal. They must have at least the legally specified minimum depth of tread and be free of dangerous cuts and defects. They must also be inflated to the right pressure.

Having your vehicle serviced at the recommended intervals will help to keep your vehicle reliable and prolong its life. Many modern vehicles will tell the driver when they require a service.

What to do in an emergency

Punctures and blow-outs (burst tyres)

If your car suddenly becomes unstable or you begin to notice steering problems, you might have a puncture or a blow-out. Try to stay calm and follow these steps.

- Do not brake suddenly.
- Take your foot off the accelerator.
- Try to keep a straight course by holding the steering wheel firmly.
- Get the vehicle away from the traffic (onto the hard shoulder if you're on a motorway).
- If you have to move the vehicle, do so very slowly to avoid further damage to the tyre or wheel rim.
- On a motorway, never attempt to change a wheel yourself. Always use one of the emergency telephones to call for help.
- On all other roads, get the vehicle to a place of safety. Before attempting repairs or changing a wheel, put on something to help passing drivers see you, such as a fluorescent jacket. At night or in poor visibility, a reflective garment is recommended.

Falling loads

If you're driving on a motorway and you see something fall from another vehicle, or if anything falls from your own vehicle, stop at the next emergency telephone and report the hazard. Do not try to retrieve the item yourself.

Vehicle fires

If your vehicle catches fire while you're driving, pull up as quickly and safely as possible. Get yourself and any passengers out and away from the vehicle. Then call the fire brigade. If the fire is under the bonnet, do not open the bonnet, as this will make the fire worse. If it's a small fire elsewhere, consider dousing it with a fire extinguisher, but avoid taking any risks.

Traffic incidents

If you're involved in a road traffic incident, you should stop whether or not it was your fault if

- another vehicle has been damaged
- someone else's property has been damaged
- someone other than yourself has been injured
- an animal that was either in another vehicle involved in the incident or in the road has been injured
- an item of street furniture – such as a sign or a lamp – has been damaged.

If you have to stop, you must give your name and address (and the name and address of the vehicle's legal owner if the car is not yours) and the registration number of the vehicle to anybody who was involved in the incident. You should also ask for the same information from any other driver(s)/persons who are affected. If you do not exchange these details at the time of the incident, you should report them to the police as soon as possible (immediately in Northern Ireland) and in any case within 24 hours.

If you break down

In the event of a breakdown

- Activate your hazard warning lights.
- Get the vehicle as far off the road as possible.
- Put on a high-visibility jacket.
- Place a warning triangle on the road, well back from the car. Note: never do this on a motorway, because it's too dangerous.
- Contact a garage or breakdown service and wait in a safe place, away from the car, for them to arrive.

On a motorway

If you break down on a motorway, steer your vehicle onto the hard shoulder or emergency area as far to the left as you can, away from the traffic. When you stop, it's a good idea to turn your wheels slightly to the left, so your vehicle is not pushed onto the main carriageway if it's hit from behind.

You should also be aware of the following procedures
- Switch on your hazard lights to warn other drivers that you've broken down.
- Make sure your sidelights are on in poor visibility or at night.
- Do not open the offside (driver's side) doors.
- Warn your passengers of the dangers of passing vehicles.
- Keep animals inside the vehicle.
- Along with your passengers, leave the vehicle by the nearside (passenger side) doors, away from the traffic. Lock all doors, except the front passenger door.
- Use the free emergency telephone to call for help. If you cannot get to the emergency telephone, use a mobile phone to call National Highways on **0300 123 5000**.
- Wait on the embankment at the other side of the crash barrier, away from the hard shoulder.

On a level crossing

If you break down on a level crossing, get everyone out of the vehicle and clear of the crossing immediately. Call the signal operator from the phone provided. Only move your vehicle if the operator tells you to do so.

 For more information on what to do if you break down, see section 15 of 'The Official DVSA Guide to Driving – the essential skills'.

safedrivingforlife.info/shop/official-dvsa-guide-driving-essential-skills

Summary

In this section, you've

- reviewed the key milestones in the development of the UK road environment
- checked your knowledge of national and local speed limits, and considered the consequences of an inappropriate choice of speed
- reflected on the way you drive on motorways and learned some techniques for safer use of these roads
- seen how to reduce the chances of a breakdown and what to do in an emergency.

2 MINUTES OF YOUR LIFE
COULD SAVE A LIFE.

SCAN THE CODE.
LEARN CPR NOW.

Section five

The way forward

In this section, you'll learn about

- how the road environment is likely to change in the coming years
- automated vehicle technology
- improving your knowledge and skills
- where to access further driver training
- a strategy for changing your driving behaviour.

What's next for UK roads?

Traffic management technology

Technology is set to have a radical impact on the way we drive and use public transport. It will reduce pollution and make vehicles easier to drive. But growth in the economy and population, and improving fuel efficiency, will increase traffic volumes.

There are currently around 38 million vehicles on the UK's roads. Limited space and resources are available to build new roads or expand existing ones, so the road network will have to 'work smarter, not harder' if widespread congestion is to be avoided. This means that we're likely to see increases in the use of traffic management technology to control the flow of traffic.

Better for the environment

Road engineers have recently focused on ways to maximise safety while minimising environmental impact. Developments are already beginning to emerge in the form of

- solar-powered cat's eyes
- glow-in-the-dark road markings
- intelligent street lights, which dim when a road is not in active use.

Self-reflection
How can you adapt to new road-engineering technology in a safe way?

What's next for UK drivers?

The challenges of increasing automation

The government considers safety to be the most important factor in planning for the introduction of automated vehicles. It's the highest priority for the agencies responsible for standards, testing and driver education.

This approach considers the safety factors involved in introducing automation, to make sure that any vehicles with these systems make drivers safer when used properly.

A lot of the terminology around vehicle automation is confusing and very technical. There's lots of research and policy background information online about formal levels of automation from assistance to self-driving. Here, we will stick to your responsibilities as the 'driver' of a car with the features that you're actually likely to see quite soon. So, for example, where technical and legal documents might use the term 'user in charge', we will use 'driver' for simplicity.

In 2023, many drivers surveyed thought that self-driving cars were already on the roads when, in fact, at the time of publication, there are **no self-driving vehicles available for the general public to buy**. However, it's likely that self-driving cars will become available soon. The government has already updated The Highway Code (2022) with a section setting out responsibilities when that happens. Additionally, the Secretary of State for Transport will publish a list of vehicles that are capable of self-driving.

 You can find a list of self-driving vehicles on this website

www.gov.uk/guidance/self-driving-vehicles-listed-for-use-in-great-britain

Eyes-on, hands-off technology

The first vehicle with 'eyes-on, hands-off' capability was introduced to UK roads in 2023. The driver may take their hands off the steering wheel, but cameras monitor them to make sure that they remain alert and watching the road, ready to take back control in an instant when needed or when they choose to. The driver is still responsible and liable for the car's actions at all times. Research shows that 'hands-off' supervision in automation mode could increase some risks; for example, when people are in the middle of a secondary task like adjusting their sat nav, they can be tempted to prioritise finishing that task over taking back control. You must understand what your car can and cannot do. The dangers are clear and a lot of work is going on to make sure that drivers' behaviour and their understanding of the technology will make the increasing levels of automation in cars safer.

If you allow yourself to be distracted; for example by listening to loud music, you might fail to monitor the system and the road properly. See distractions on pages 20 to 21 and 59 to 65 and see also section 3 (ADAS) of Driving Essential Skills.

Next-level automation

The next level of vehicle autonomy to appear on our roads after ADAS will be automatic lane-keeping systems (ALKS). This will be the first of a generation of vehicles that is capable of driving without the driver's input to the steering wheel or pedals. When speeds and conditions are right on dual carriageways and motorways, the vehicle may offer to engage ALKS through the instrument display. If the driver chooses to accept, the system can operate the vehicle using

- sensors
- cameras
- radar and light detection and ranging (LiDAR) technology.

On certain roads and at certain speeds, the system allows the vehicle to process the information about its environment and then take the necessary action. This will include lane-keeping, stopping, starting, manoeuvring or changing speed. That is much more advanced and quite different from lane-keeping assist, which is covered in the section on new technologies on pages 76 to 86.

Essential safety strategies

When using a car with features like ALKS, you
- must never remove your seat belt
- must be sober and fit to drive
- must not use a hand-held mobile phone.

It's more important than ever to keep up to date with your understanding of The Highway Code in these and other matters. You can use The Official DVSA Highway Code app for this, or subscribe to email alerts about changes to **www.gov.uk/highway-code**

Adjusting your seat or steering wheel from your comfortable driving position adds unnecessary risk and delay when you have to set it back again to take over control. The system will request you to take back control by using
- the displays
- the sound system
- sensory alerts, such as vibrations in your seat, seat belt, steering wheel or pedals.

You must assess the conditions and your surroundings quickly and take back control promptly.

You should stay ready to take back control if needed. It's a good idea to make some checks of where you are on your journey, so that you have an idea of when you might expect a takeover request. The vehicle may request that you take back control at any time, and if you're not able to check all around, get ready and take control of the wheel and pedals in time, the car will come to a rapid but controlled stop. That could be dangerous, as other road users will not expect this, and you may be liable for any resulting incident.

Research shows that there are potential unintended consequences of such automation. It's very easy to lose concentration or to 'zone out' when the car is driving itself. You must be aware of the risk of over-relying on the system. Being 'out of the loop' and unaware when the vehicle needs you to take over is also potentially dangerous. You may only have a few seconds in which to respond to a takeover request.

What is a takeover request?

When a vehicle is in a mode such as ALKS, it may issue a takeover request at any time.

A takeover request may be issued for a number of reasons, including
- the road type is changing to one that's unsuitable for the system
- heavy traffic
- complex road environments
- the lane markings or road signs that systems rely on are unclear
- bad weather
- the sensors are obscured
- the sensors miscategorise an event or object
- the sensors fail to respond
- the sensors cannot tell if the conditions suitable for it to function are ending.

The steps in a takeover request

You should always know where you are in your journey, and be ready for when you'll need to take back control. You should not rely on the system to warn you. But, for safety and in case of anything unanticipated, the vehicle might give an early warning of changing conditions ahead that are likely to need you to take over control. If you get such a warning, the vehicle will give you at least 10 seconds before you must take control; but, remember, you may not have 10 seconds to react. This is because your speed and distance from the reason for the takeover request may require you to take over sooner.

There are 3 steps to taking over control of the vehicle.
- Step 1: The vehicle issues a takeover request with a sound and visual alert through a display and sound system. There may also be a sensory or haptic cue, such as a vibration in the driver's seat or seat belt tensioner. This will give you 10 seconds, if possible. It continues to give warnings with increasing urgency until step 3.
- Step 2: While the car is in takeover mode, you quickly
  - ignore any other distractions and prepare to focus on the driving task by looking all around you and using your mirrors to assess other traffic, judge distances and consider the road conditions
  - get yourself into your driving position, finding the pedals with your feet, and the steering wheel and the other controls with your hands. Importantly, you must never remove your seat belt at any stage

- Step 3: You take over manual control and either switch off the system or the system itself confirms when it has stopped.

If you do not respond to the request quickly enough; for example, because you complete another task before taking back control, the vehicle will quickly come to a controlled stop. That could be very serious, especially as these systems are designed for faster roads, such as motorways and dual carriageways. It's surprisingly common for drivers to be unable to find the right pedals after distractions, especially lengthy interruptions; therefore, making a conscious effort is advised.

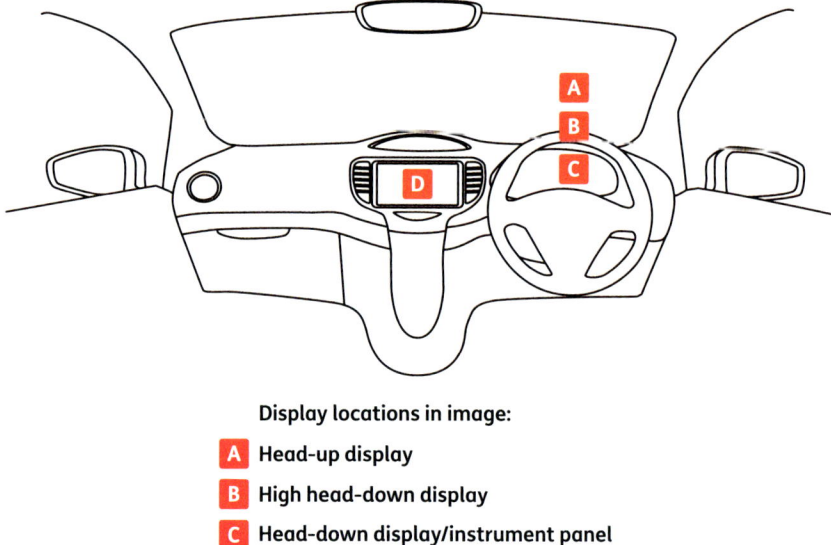

Display locations in image:
- **A** Head-up display
- **B** High head-down display
- **C** Head-down display/instrument panel
- **D** Centre console

Takeover requests might use any or all of the car's visual displays, as well as sounds and vibrations

Automated technology and your driving skills

As automation increases, drivers at any stage in their driving lives will have less opportunity to develop their driving skills. As a result, your experience and skills will not increase as quickly compared with driving in fully manual mode. That means you should regularly reflect on your skills and use strategies to address skill decay.

Your mind links patterns and actions (steering and braking, for example) with certain situations on the road. These links form the basis of skilled driving, and they're more likely to fade if they're not practised. This 'skill decay' has a stronger impact on skills such as decision making and hazard perception. This results in more errors of judgement and an increase in reaction time. We should remain aware that automation of driving may interfere with our manual driving skills.

Strategies for safe driving

Here are some techniques that can help you to overcome the effects of skill decay.

- If you notice that your driving skills are fading when the system asks you to take over (or when you're driving an older vehicle with limited ADAS features), the best way to refresh your manual skills is to contact a local DVSA-approved driving instructor. Their expert feedback will improve your driving.
- Hazard perception training can improve cognitive skills in driving.
- Commentary drives can improve hazard perception skills.

Commentary drives are when you give a brief verbal commentary of the emerging hazards while you're driving. This helps you to stay focused on what's happening around your vehicle. It has been found to

- improve hazard perception test scores
- increase scanning to the left and right during driving
- lead to better speed control when approaching hazards.

You can practise this skill before you try it behind the wheel by watching video clips from the driver's perspective and giving a brief commentary of the emerging hazards you can see.

 There are free tests available on the Safe Driving for Life website to help you improve your awareness of hazards.

safedrivingforlife.info/free-practice-tests/ hazard-perception-test

An ongoing process

Being a safe and competent driver is a life-long affair. As you progress through your driving career, your driving may be tested in a number of different situations, including

- as a driver at work
- as a new parent
- as a driver under pressure
- as you get older
- as you experience life-changing events
- as a convicted driver
- as the road environment changes
- as traffic conditions change
- as the vehicles you drive change.

Reflecting on your strengths and weaknesses will help you to find ways to deal with these situations and improve your driving. With a small amount of effort, you can make big changes and increase your awareness of your driving behaviour with every trip.

Additional help

The Highway Code

We've seen how developments in the road environment, legislation and vehicle technology can have an impact on your driving. In section 4, we looked at some of the key changes that have taken place over the past 60 years, but there have been many more. Read the latest edition of 'The Official Highway Code' for an up-to-date guide to road signs and traffic rules that you may not be aware of.

facebook.com/HighwayCodeGB

www.gov.uk/highway-code

www.gov.uk/the-highway-code/updates

instagram.com/safe.driving.for.life

Developing your practical skills

Hazard perception training

Even though you may have had years of driving experience, you're unlikely to have received any additional training to improve your hazard perception skills since you passed your driving test. This is important, because even a small amount of hazard perception training leads to significant increases in your ability to respond to hazards while driving.

For more help and advice on developing your hazard perception skills, see 'The Official DVSA Guide to Hazard Perception Online' and 'The Official DVSA Guide to Driving – the essential skills'.

Take a free practice theory test, and a road signs quiz, at this website.

safedrivingforlife.info/free-practice-tests

 Did you know The Official DVSA Guide to Better Driving is also available as an e-learning course?

safedrivingforlife.info/shop/the-official-dvsa-better-driving-elearning-course

Further driver training

Throughout this book, we've suggested that taking lessons with an approved driving instructor (ADI) may help you to refresh your skills and get some practical guidance behind the wheel.

Some ADIs have received specialist training on the human factors in driving and have developed their ability to address many of the concerns you may have about your driving, in a practical one-to-one environment. This is referred to as client-centred learning or driver coaching.

 You can find your nearest ADI on GOV.UK.

www.gov.uk/find-driving-schools-and-lessons

You can also develop your driving by getting in touch with one of the following organisations to find some advanced training that suits your needs.

The AA
Go to **http://www.theaa.com/driving-school/qualified-driver-lessons** or call **0330 100 7474**.
Whether you've just passed or are more experienced, book refresher qualified driver lessons to practise any driving skills (general, town driving, all-weather driving, out-of-town driving and rural roads, night driving, dual carriageways, motorway driving). If you're a new driver, take the six-hour Pass Plus course to gain confidence and experience on the roads.

DIAmond Advanced Motorists
Go to **advancedmotoring.co.uk/** or call **020 8686 8010**.
A DIAmond Advanced Instructor can familiarise you with the requirements of the test and give you feedback to work on. The hour-long test is objectively scored, going beyond style and technique to reflect a commitment to driving in a way that saves fuel, minimises wear and tear, and stresses forward planning and anticipation. No special techniques are needed, but fuel-efficient driving means gentle acceleration, avoiding jerky car control and planning manoeuvres well in advance.

IAM RoadSmart (formerly the Institute of Advanced Motorists)
Go to **iamroadsmart.com/local-groups** and enter your postcode for your local group or call **0300 303 1134**.
The advanced driver courses provide you with everything you need to pass the advanced driving test, and when you pass you'll become a full member of IAM RoadSmart. There are over 200 local volunteer groups and yours will support you in preparing for the test. Included in the fee is 12 months' membership of IAM RoadSmart and *RoadSmart*, the members-only magazine.

Royal Society for the Prevention of Accidents (RoSPA)
Go to **rospa.com/shop/products/roadar-driving-review**
The RoADAR Driving Review is a simple and low-cost way for people who have been driving for some time to find out whether their driving skills are up to scratch.
The review is taken in your own car and lasts 45 to 60 minutes, with the reviewer giving feedback throughout the review. You also receive a written report, usually within 2 weeks.

Self-reflection

Have you received any further driver training or education since passing your driving test?

How do you think your driving has changed since you learned to drive?

About 80% of drivers believe they're better than the average driver. What does this suggest?

Changing your driving behaviour

Throughout this book, we've seen that improving your driving judgement, knowledge and skills starts with increasing your awareness of the human factors that affect the way you drive. As a final exercise, think about the following process of behavioural change and try to work out which stage you're at. Each stage will have its own difficulties and obstacles to overcome, but with a little time, effort and application, you'll find that your driving confidence really can improve.

Stage 1: Precontemplation (Not ready to change)

You're unaware that your behaviour is problematic, and you're not thinking about making any change.

Think about accessing information from reliable sources to increase your awareness of what's at stake.

Stage 2: Contemplation (Getting ready)

You're beginning to recognise that something needs to change to improve your driving behaviour. You look at the pros and cons involved.

You've read this book. Now think about what's at stake if you do not make a change, and what you can gain if you do make a change.

Stage 3: Preparation (Ready to change)

You intend to take action to improve your driving, and you may begin to take small steps towards a change.

Think about the advice contained in this book and develop some manageable goals over the next few weeks. Do not try to do too much at once; instead, take small steps towards your ultimate goal. Develop an action plan to help you achieve it.

Stage 4: Taking action

You're making specific modifications to your behaviour, and you're learning new and safer ways of driving.

You're now implementing your action plan. Do not be put off if it takes a little time to see an improvement in your driving. Keep trying. Think about how you need to build on your successes; notice even small improvements and congratulate yourself on them.

Stage 5: Maintenance

You've been able to see a steady improvement over time, and you're focused on making sure you keep it up.

If you have a bad day and return to your old ways, do not be disheartened. Refocus and move on. You know you can do it. Think about how you can continue to improve by selecting and working on different aspects of your driving. It's time to think about a new set of goals.

> **! Remember**
> You can meet the challenge of changing your driving behaviour and improving your driving abilities if you believe you can. Imagine how good you'll feel when you're driving better. With the right motivation and a bit of persistence, you'll be surprised by how much you can achieve in a short space of time.

Driver & Vehicle Standards Agency

Safe Driving for Life

The Official DVSA Better Driving e-learning course

Take your learning further with **interactive activities, video exercises, summary quizzes and more**.

Stay safe: understand how your thoughts and feelings impact driving.

Boost confidence: advice on coping with roundabouts, motorways, bad weather and more.

Enjoy driving: evaluate and improve your safety and performance.

Stay legal: keep up to date with the latest rules on speed, drink-/drug-driving and mobile phones.

e-learning for business

Better Driving e-learning can be used by any organisation looking to improve the safety of their drivers and riders.

For more information, check out
www.safedrivingforlife.info/shop/multi-user-access/

Save 10%*

Order online at **safedrivingforlife.info/shop** quoting **SD10** at the checkout, or call **01603 696979** quoting **SD10** to receive **10%** discount.

 safedrivinglife   safedrivingforlifeinfo   safe.driving.for.life   safe.driving.for.life

TSO (The Stationery Office) is proud to be DVSA's official publishing partner. TSO pays for the marketing of all the products we publish. Images are correct at time of going to press but subject to change without notice. The Stationery Office Limited is registered in England No. 3049649 at 18 Central Avenue, St Andrews Business Park, Norwich, NR7 0HR. * Please note smartphone apps and e-books are not included in the promotional discount.

Photographic credits

Section one

Page 12 – Man looking in rear-view mirror
George Doyle/Stockbyte/Thinkstock

Page 20 – Think! emoji poster
Think! Road Safety/Department for Transport

Page 43 – Car on rural road
National Highways

Page 47 – Female's hand using GPS navigation
Andrey Popov/Adobe Stock

Section two

Page 62 – Car radio
Adobe Stock

Page 63 – Family in car
Mark Bowden/iStock/Thinkstock

Page 87 – Road widening
National Highways

Page 87 – Tunnel
National Highways

Section three

Page 101 – Child in car seat with teddy
Jupiterimages/BananaStock/Thinkstock

Page 103 – Motorway at dusk
Krzysztof Melech/iStock/Thinkstock

Page 104 – Cars driving on motorway in wet weather
National Highways

Page 111 – Traffic light
Jupiterimages/Polka Dot/Thinkstock

Page 111 – Speed camera
Ashley Pickering/iStock/Thinkstock

Section four

Page 120 – Pile of UK road signs
Creisinger/iStock/Thinkstock

Page 121 – 1960s policeman breathalysing member of the public
Courtesy of Greater Manchester Police Museum and Archives

Page 123 – Police enforcement camera
Mark Richardson/Hemera/Thinkstock

Page 132 – National speed limit sign
Martin Meehan/iStock/Thinkstock

Page 140 – Hand on mop
Andrey Popov/iStock/Thinkstock

Appendix: The national standard for driving

The national standard for driving describes the skills, knowledge and understanding you need to be a safe and responsible driver of a car or light van.

Based on extensive research and consultation, the standard is the basis for the driving test and all the official learning materials that DVSA publishes for drivers, at every stage of their driving career.

The standard is split into 5 sections, or 'roles', and each role covers a different aspect of driving a car or light van.

Each of these roles is then broken down into units, which cover specific areas within each role.

The units are further broken down into elements, which cover
- what you must be able to do
- what you must know and understand.

The full national standard can be found at **www.gov.uk**, but the following table sets out
- the 5 roles
- their units
- an example of an element and what you'll need to know and understand in that element.

Role 1	Prepare yourself, the vehicle and its passengers for a journey
Unit 1.1	Prepare yourself and passengers for a journey
	Element 1.1.2 Make sure you're fit to drive You must be able to assess whether your ability to drive safely and legally is affected by your emotional state, a short- or long-term physical condition, or tiredness. You must know and understand what the law says about driving while you have illegal or controlled substances or alcohol in your system.
Unit 1.2	Make sure the vehicle is roadworthy
Unit 1.3	Plan a journey
Role 2	**Guide and control the vehicle**
Unit 2.1	Start, move off, stop and leave the vehicle safely and responsibly
Unit 2.2	Drive the vehicle safely and responsibly
	Element 2.2.4 Steer the vehicle safely You must be able to steer the vehicle safely and responsibly in all road and traffic conditions. You must know and understand how to keep safe control of the steering wheel.
Unit 2.3	Drive the vehicle while towing a trailer or caravan
Role 3	**Use the road in accordance with The Highway Code**
Unit 3.1	Negotiate the road correctly
	Element 3.1.4 Drive on motorways and dual carriageways You must be able to drive in the most suitable lane. You must know and understand that you may not stop on a motorway except in an emergency.
Unit 3.2	Comply with signals, signs and road markings

Role 4	Drive safely and responsibly in the traffic system
Unit 4.1	Interact correctly with other road users
Unit 4.2	Minimise risk when driving
	Element 4.2.2 Drive defensively You must be able to create and maintain a safe driving space. You must know and understand the importance of keeping a safe separation distance in all weather and traffic conditions.
Unit 4.3	Manage incidents effectively
Role 5	**Review and adjust driving behaviour over lifetime**
Unit 5.1	Learn from experience
	Element 5.1 Learn from experience You must be able to show that you have continued to develop and update your driving skills since you took your driving test. You must know and understand that you can learn from experience and continue to improve your ability to drive safely and responsibly all through your driving career.
Unit 5.2	Keep up to date with changes

Role 5 – which states that you need to review and adjust your driving behaviour over your lifetime, by learning from experience and keeping up to date with changes – will influence everything you do in roles 1–4.

Self-evaluation through reflective thinking – as you've been doing throughout this book – will help you to develop greater self-awareness. Being self-aware means that you're more likely to take responsibility for your actions.

The whole process is about identifying your strengths and limitations, and tracing these back to the way you think and feel. In this way, you'll be better able to manage your behaviour and develop strategies to cope with the driving situations you typically find challenging.

Selected bibliography

This is a selective list of the main sources drawn on to compile the statistics and information in this book.

Section 2

Department for Transport (DfT) (2020). *Reported road casualties in Great Britain: provisional estimates involving illegal alcohol levels: 2018.*
www.gov.uk/government/statistics/reported-road-casualties-in-great-britain-provisional-estimates-involving-illegal-alcohol-levels-2018

Section 4

Bayliss, D. (2009). *Accident trends by road type.* RAC Foundation.

Chris's British Road Directory. cbrd.co.uk (now Roads.org.uk)

DfT (2013). *Action for Roads: A network for the 21st century.* HMSO.

DfT (2019). *Reported Road Casualties in Great Britain 2018.*
www.gov.uk/government/statistics/reported-road-casualties-in-great-britain-annual-report-2018

Driver and Vehicle Licensing Agency (DVLA) (2006). *A Brief History of Registration.* DVLA/DfT report INF57.

Keep, M. and Rutherford, T. (2013). *Reported Road Accident Statistics.* House of Commons Library, Social and General Statistics Section, Note SN/SG/2198.

International Transport Forum (ITF) and International Traffic Safety Data and Analysis Group (IRTAD) (2021), Sweden: Road safety country profile, 2021: The impact of Covid-19. itf-oecd.org/sites/default/files/sweden-road-safety.pdf

Leibling, D. (2008). *Car Ownership in Great Britain.* RAC Foundation.

Organisation for Economic Co-operation and Development (OECD) (1990). *Behavioural Adaptations to Changes in the Road Transport System*, Paris: OECD, Road Transport Research, 5.

Rosenbloom, S. (2001). Sustainability and automobility among the elderly: an international assessment. *Transportation*, 28, 375–408.

Statistics Norway (2024). Road traffic accidents involving personal injury. 12043: Persons killed or severely injured in road traffic accidents 1946–2023. www.ssb.no/en/statbank/table/12043/

All other sections

Aschenbrenner, K.M. and Biehl, B. (1994). Improved safety through improved technical measures? *Challenges to Accident Prevention. The Issue of Risk Compensation Behaviour,* 81–9.

Canalys Estimates for UK ADAS (2021). Retrieved from canalys.com/newsroom/huge-opportunity-as-only-10-of-the-1-billion-cars-in-use-have-adas-features

Chapman, P. and Groeger, J.A. (2004). Risk and the recognition of driving situations. Applied Cognitive Psychology, 18, 1–19.

Chapman, P., Underwood, G. and Roberts, K. (2002). Visual search patterns in trained and untrained novice drivers. *Transportation Research Part F: Traffic Psychology and Behaviour,* 5(2), 157–67.

Crundall, D., Andrews, B., van Loon, E. and Chapman, P. (2010). Commentary training improves responsiveness to hazards in a driving simulator. *Accident Analysis & Prevention,* 42(6), 2117–24.

Crundall, D. and Underwood, G. (1998). The effects of experience and processing demands on visual information acquisition in drivers. *Ergonomics*, 41, 448–58.

Crundall, D., Underwood, G. and Chapman, P. (2002). Attending to the peripheral world while driving. *Applied Cognitive Psychology*, 16, 459–75.

Dorn, L. and Matthews, G. (1992). Two further studies of personality correlates of driver stress. *Personality and Individual Differences*, 13, 949–51.

Dorn, L. and Matthews, G. (1995). Prediction of mood and risk appraisals from trait measures: two studies of simulated driving. *European Journal of Personality*, 9, 25–42.

Eriksson, A. and Stanton, N.A. (2017). Takeover time in highly automated vehicles: Noncritical transitions to and from manual control. *Human Factors*, 59(4), 689–705.

Fairclough, S.H., Tattersall, A.J. and Houston, K. (2006). Anxiety and performance in the British driving test. *Transportation Research Part F: Traffic Psychology and Behaviour,* 9(1), 43–52.

Furlan, A.D., Kajaks, T., Tiong, M., Lavallière, M., Campos, J. L., Babineau, J., Haghzare, S., Ma, T. and Vrkljan, B. (2020). Advanced vehicle technologies and road safety: A scoping review of the evidence. *Accident Analysis & Prevention*, 147, 105741.

Gregersen, N.P. (1996). Young drivers' overestimation of their own skill – an experiment on the relation between training strategy and skill. *Accident Analysis and Prevention*, 28(2), 243–50.

Guo, F. and Fang, Y. (2013). Individual driver risk assessment using naturalistic driving data. *Accident Analysis and Prevention*, 61, 3–9.

Hatakka, M., Keskinen, E., Gregersen, N.P., Glad, A. and Hernetkoski, K. (2002). From control of the vehicle to personal self-control; broadening the perspectives to driver education. *Transportation Research Part F*, 5, 201–15.

Helman, S. and Carsten, O. (2019). *What Does My Car Do?* Parliamentary Advisory Council for Transport Safety (PACTS).

Hoedemaeker, M. and Brookhuis, K.A. (1998). Behavioural adaptation to driving with an adaptive cruise control (ACC). *Transportation Research Part F: Traffic Psychology and Behaviour,* 1(2), 95–106.

Horne, J.A. and Reyner, L.A. (1995). Sleep related vehicle accidents. *British Medical Journal*, 310, 565–7.

International Energy Agency (2019). *Global EV Outlook*. Paris, France.

Isler, R.B., Starkey, N.J. and Williamson, A.R. (2009). Video-based road commentary training improves hazard perception of young drivers in a dual task. *Accident Analysis & Prevention,* 41(3), 445–52.

Kathiresh, M. and Neelaveni, R. (2021). *Automotive Embedded Systems: Key technologies, innovations, and applications.* EAII/Springer Innovations in Communication and Computing. springer.com/series/15427

Lajunen, T. and Summala, H. (1995). Driving experience, personality, and skill and safety-motive dimensions in drivers' self-assessments. *Personality and Individual Differences*, 19, 307–18.

Lee, C. and Abdel-Aty, M. (2008). Presence of passengers: Does it increase or reduce driver's crash potential? *Accident Analysis & Prevention*, 40, 1703–12.

Lerner N.D., Harpster J.L., Huey R.W. and Steinberg, G.V. (1997). Driver backing-behavior research: Implications for backup warning devices. *Transportation Research Record,* 1573(1), 23–9.

Litman, T. (2017). *Autonomous vehicle implementation predictions.* Canada: Victoria Transport Policy Institute.

Matthews, G. (2002). Towards a transactional ergonomics for driver stress and fatigue. *Theoretical Issues in Ergonomic Science,* 3, 195–211.

Matthews, G., Dorn, L., Hoyes, T.W., Davies, D.R., Glendon, A.I. and Taylor, R.G. (1998). Driver stress and performance on a driving simulator. *Human Factors,* 40, 136–49.

Maycock, G. (1997). *The safety of older car-drivers in the European Union.* European Road Safety Federation, ERSF, AA Foundation for Road Safety Research, Basingstoke, UK.

Miller, E.E. and Ng Boyle, L. (2019). Behavioral adaptations to lane keeping systems: Effects of exposure and withdrawal. *Human Factors,* 61(1), 152–64.

Monfort, S.S., Reagan, I.J., Cicchino, J.B., Wen Hu., Gershon, P., Mehler, B. and Reimer, B. (2022). Speeding behavior while using adaptive cruise control and lane centering in free flow traffic, *Traffic Injury Prevention,* 23(2), 85–90.

Morris, J. (2017). Drink drive figures: cause for concern in 2017? www.alcoholpolicy.net/2017/10/drink-drive-figures-cause-for-concern-2017.html

OECD (2006). *Young Drivers: The road to safety.* Organisation for Economic Co-operation and Development. European Conference of Ministers of Transport.

Oviedo-Trespalacios, O., Tichon, J. and Briant, O. (2021). Is a flick-through enough? A content analysis of Advanced Driver Assistance Systems (ADAS) user manuals. *PLoS ONE,* 16(6), e0252688.

Poldrack, R.A., Sabb, F.W., Foerde, K., Tom, S.M., Asarnow, R.F., Bookheimer, S.Y. and Knowlton, B.J. (2005). The neural correlates of motor skill automaticity. *Journal of Neuroscience,* 25(22), 5356–64.

Rudin-Brown, C., Burns, P., Hagen, L., Roberts, S. and Scipione, A. (2012). Behavioural adaptation as a consequence of extended use of low-speed backing aids. In Sullman, M. and Dorn, L. (eds), *Advances in Traffic Psychology.* Ashgate, Burlington, VT, 285–94.

Rudin-Brown, C.M. and Parker, H.A. (2004). Behavioural adaptation to adaptive cruise control (ACC): implications for preventive strategies. *Transportation Research Part F: Traffic Psychology and Behaviour,* 7(2), 59–76.

Sabey, B.E. and Taylor, H. (1980). The known risks we run: the highway. In Schwing, R.C. and Albers, W.A., Jr. (eds), *Societal Risk Assessment: How Safe is Safe Enough?* Plenum Press, New York.

Sagberg, F., Fosser, S. and Sätermo, I.-A. (1997). An investigation of behavioural adaptation to airbags and antilock brakes among taxi drivers. *Accident Analysis and Prevention,* 29, 293–302.

Seow, R. Y. T., Betts, S. A. and Anderson, J. R. (2021). A decay-based account of learning and adaptation in complex skills. *Journal of Experimental Psychology: Learning, Memory, and Cognition,* 47(11), 1761–91.

Stern, E. (1999). Reactions to congestion under time pressure. *Transportation Research Part C*, 7, 75–90.

Underwood, G., Chapman, P., Bowden, K. and Crundall, D. (2002). Visual search while driving: Skill and awareness during inspection of the scene. *Transportation Research Part F*, 5, 87–97.

Underwood, G., Crundall, D. and Chapman, P. (2002). Selective searching while driving: The role of experience in hazard detection and general surveillance. *Ergonomics*, 45, 1–12.

Upahita, D.P., Wong, Y.D. and Lum, K.M. (2018). Effect of driving experience and driving inactivity on young driver's hazard mitigation skills. *Transportation Research Part F: Traffic Psychology and Behaviour,* 59, 286–97.

Vogelpohl, T., Gehlmann, F. and Vollrath, M. (2020). Task interruption and control recovery strategies after take-over requests emphasize need for measures of situation awareness. *Human Factors,* 62(7), 1190–211.

Webster, E. and Davies, D. (2020) *What Kills Most on the Roads?* (2nd edn). Parliamentary Advisory Council for Transport Safety (PACTS).

Wegman, F., Johnston, I., Kroj, R. and Pain, R. (2007). *Road Traffic Safety Research and Education in Israel*. Ramat Hasharon: The Ran Naor Foundation for the Advancement of Road Safety Research.

Zhang, B., de Winter, J., Varotto, S., Happee, R. and Martens, M. (2019). Determinants of take-over time from automated driving: A meta-analysis of 129 studies. *Transportation Research Part F: Traffic Psychology and Behaviour,* 64, 285–307.

Questionnaires

Lajunen, T. and Summala, H. (1995). Driving experience, personality, and skill and safety-motive dimensions in drivers' self-assessment. Personality and Individual Differences, 19, 307–18.

Lawton, R.J., Parker, D., Manstead, A.S.R. and Stradling, S.G. (1997). The role of affect in predicting social behaviours: The case of road traffic violations. Journal of Applied Social Psychology, 27, 1258–76.

Matthews, G., Desmond, P.A., Joyner, L., Carcary, B. and Gilliland, K. (1997). A comprehensive questionnaire measure of driver stress and affect. In Rothengatter, T. and Vaya, E.C., *Traffic and Transport Psychology: Theory and Application*, 317–24. Amsterdam: Pergamon.

McKenna, F.P. (1993). It won't happen to me. Unrealistic optimism or illusion of control? *British Journal of Psychology*, 84, 39–50.

Index

AA 158
ABS (anti-lock braking systems) 78, 80–1, 85
accidents 142
adaptive cruise control 78, 84, 86
ADIs (approved driving instructors) 157
advanced driver assistance systems (ADAS) 78–86
age and driving 20, 113–15
alcohol 69–71
anger 24, 49–55
anti-lock braking systems (ABS) 78, 80–1, 85
anxiety 91–4, 108–10
approved driving instructors (ADIs) 157
automation 79, 83–6, 148–9, 153
Automobile Association (AA) 158

behaviour, driving 9, 23–5, 40–4, 159–60
beliefs 24–5
blind spots 22, 137
blow-outs 141
brain processes 16–19, 21–2, 36, 93
braking distance 17
breakdowns 142–3
breathalysers 69–70
burst tyres 141

children 64, 101–2
collision avoidance systems 83
collisions 21–2, 28, 31–2, 66, 142
confidence 33–9
convictions, driving 37–9, 111–12
coping strategies 47–8, 114, 117
cruise control 78, 84, 86
cyclists 107, 127–9

dazzle 103
deaths on the road 121
defensive driving 13–14
DIAmond Advanced Motorists 158
distractions 20–1, 59–65
drink-driving 69–71
driver assistance systems, advanced (ADAS) 78–86
driver training 157–9
driving offences 37–9, 111–12
driving test 121–5
drugs 71–5

eating and drinking 64
electric vehicles 76–7
entertainment systems 62–3
environmental impact 147
errors 37–9

falling loads 141
fatigue 66–8
fear reactions 93
feedback 26
feeling and thinking 23–5
field impairment assessment (FIA) 71
fires, vehicle 142
food and drink 64
fuel tanks 140

goods vehicles, heavy 137

'hardy' individuals 93
hazard perception 16–19, 49, 153–4, 156
headlights 102–3
heavy goods vehicles (HGVs) 137
hierarchy of road users 127–9
Highway Code, The 127–9, 155–6

IAM RoadSmart 158
ice 105
illegal drugs 73
in-car entertainment systems 62–3
incidents, traffic 142
intelligent parking assistance 79, 114

junctions 21–2, 95–6, 129

lane-keeping assist 78, 86, 149
lanes 98, 135–6, 137, 138
lapses 37–9
law, breaking the 37–9, 111–12
learner drivers 108–10
'legal highs' 73
level crossings 143
lights 102–3, 140
loads, falling 141
local speed limits 132
long journeys 99

maintenance, vehicle 100, 140–1
medication 70, 73–5
mental processes 15–18, 21–2, 36, 93
'microsleeps' 67
mobile phones 59–61
motorcyclists 107
motorway service areas 68
motorways 135–9, 143
music in cars 62–3

naps 67, 68
national speed limits 130–4
nervousness 25, 91–4, 99
night driving 102–3

offences, driving 37–9, 111–12
older drivers 20, 113–15
optimism bias 29–32
overconfidence 33–6

parking 106
parking assistance 79, 114
passengers 63–4
personal safety margins 28–9
personality 40–4
pessimistic bias 29
physiological changes 93
prescription drugs 73–5
punctures 141

radios, car 62–3
rain 104
reaction time 17, 18
rest breaks 67–8
risk perception 28–32
risk-taking behaviour 40–4
road deaths 121
road engineering 87–8
road layout 46
road users, hierarchy of 127–9
roundabouts 96–8
Royal Society for the Prevention of Accidents (RoSPA) 158

safe system approach 125–6
safety bubbles 28–9
satellite navigation (sat nav) systems 61–2, 83
self-driving vehicles 78, 148
self-reflection 26–7, 39
sensation-seeking behaviour 40–4
servicing, vehicle 140–1
shared-space zones 88
skidding 105
skills, driving 9, 23–5, 36, 115
  automated technology 153
sleep apnoea 67
snow 105
speed limits 130–4
speeding 111, 133–4
spiral roundabouts 97
stopping distance 17
stress 45–8, 93–4, 108–10, 116–18

takeover requests 151–2
thinking and feeling 23–5
thinking distance 17
thrill-seeking behaviour 40–3
time pressure 46–8
tiredness 66–8
traffic incidents 142
traffic management technology 138, 147

traffic offences 37–9, 111–12
training, driver 157–9
tyres 141

unfamiliar roads 99

variable speed limits 133, 138
vehicle maintenance 100, 140–1
violations 37–9, 111–12

wet weather 104

young drivers 20

Learner driver insurance

£275 for cover on your parents' Fiat 500*

Text QUOTEME to 82228

Reasons to insure with Adrian Flux

- Comprehensive policies available for vehicles up to insurance group 45. Policies can be arranged on either your own car or a policy in your name on a parent's car.

- Any claim will be settled on the learner driver's insurance policy and will not affect the no claims bonus of the vehicle owner's insurance.**

- Cover can be taken out on a month-by-month basis, so you only pay for the cover you need before passing your test.

- If you're a twin there's no need to pay double – we can add twins to the same vehicle and it might not even increase your premium!

We are not on comparison websites! Get our best rates by calling 0344 3817 830

Call our UK team on 0344 3817 830
Authorised & regulated by the Financial Conduct Authority

adrianflux.co.uk/learner-drivers

*Based on a 17 year old learner driver taking out an annual policy
**If the vehicle belongs to someone else

ADRIAN FLUX
Insurance for the individual

Safe Driving for Life

 Driver & Vehicle Standards Agency

Personalise your driving journey with official DVSA learning tools

Everyone learns differently – that's why official DVSA products are available in a format that suits you. From your theory test, right through to increasing your confidence on the road, we have a book, e-learning course or app just for you.

Get 10% off using code SD10* at checkout

Over 90% of people who used our Safe Driving for Life e-learning platform passed their theory test!**

Official DVSA e-learning
Our courses are packed full of interactive activities with subscription lengths that suit you.

Official DVSA books
Our books provide all the information you need to drive safely and sustainably for life.

To find out more about our range, scan the QR code or visit **safedrivingforlife.info**

Official DVSA apps
Do you have 10 minutes to spare? With the official apps, you can learn while you're on the go and from the palm of your hand.

Visit the app storefront to view all our apps

 safedrivinglife   safedrivingforlifeinfo   safe.driving.for.life   safe.driving.for.life

TSO (The Stationery Office) is proud to be DVSA's official publishing partner. TSO pays for the marketing of all the products we publish. Images are correct at time of going to press but subject to change without notice. The Stationery Office Limited is registered in England No. 3049649 at 18 Central Avenue, St Andrews Business Park, Norwich, NR7 0HR. * Please note smartphone apps and e-books are not included in the promotional discount. ** This statistic is verified by an ongoing customer feedback survey.

Published by TSO (The Stationery Office), part of Williams Lea, and available from:

Online
www.tsoshop.co.uk

Mail, Telephone & E-mail
TSO
PO Box 29, Norwich, NR3 1GN
Telephone orders/General enquiries: 0333 202 5070
E-mail: customer.services@tso.co.uk
Textphone: 0333 202 5077